THE
CHEMISTRY

FOOD OF

CARLA MOONEY

Illustrated by Traci Van Wagoner

Nomad Press

A division of Nomad Communications

10 9 8 7 6 5 4 3 2 1

This book was manufactured by CGB Printers,
North Mankato, Minnesota, United States
August 2021, Job #1024083

ISBN Softcover: 978-1-64741-026-1
ISBN Hardcover: 978-1-64741-023-0

Educational Consultant, Marla Conn

Questions regarding the ordering of this book should be addressed to
Nomad Press
PO Box 1036, Norwich, VT 05055
www.nomadpress.net

Printed in the United States.

More chemistry titles from Nomad Press

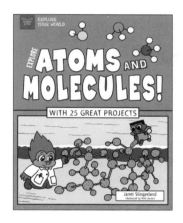

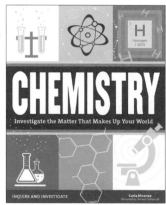

Check out more titles at www.nomadpress.net

You can use a smartphone or tablet app to scan the QR codes and explore more! Cover up neighboring QR codes to make sure you're scanning the right one. You can find a list of URLs on the Resources page.

If the QR code doesn't work, try searching the internet with the Keyword Prompts to find other helpful sources.

Interested in primary sources? **Look for this icon.**

food chemistry

Contents

TIMELINE

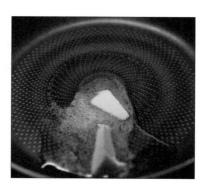

460–370 BCE: Democritus of Ancient Greece introduces the idea of matter in the form of particles, which he calls atoms. He proposes that all matter is made of these tiny units.

300 BCE: Aristotle of Ancient Greece declares that there are only four elements: fire, air, water, and earth. He believes that all matter is made from these four elements.

1000s: Ancient Egyptians extract flavors and scents from plants in the form of essential oils.

1787: Antoine Laurent Lavoisier publishes his system for classifying and naming chemical substances. He is later known as the father of chemistry.

1851: The first artificially flavored candy is displayed in the chemistry section of the Great Exhibition in the Crystal Palace in London, England.

1869: Dmitri Mendeleev publishes the first modern periodic table to classify elements. The table allows scientists to predict the properties of undiscovered elements.

1898: J.J. Thomson discovers the electron.

1906: U.S. President Theodore Roosevelt signs the Pure Food and Drug Act into law, making it illegal to produce, sell, or transport food or drugs that are poisonous or mislabeled. All imitation flavors in food must be labeled.

1908: The flavor umami is first identified by Kikunae Ikeda, a professor of the Tokyo Imperial University.

1911: Ernest Rutherford, Hans Geiger, and Ernest Marsden prove the nuclear model of the atom, which has a small, dense, positively charged nucleus surrounded by an electron cloud.

1913: Niels Bohr proposes the Bohr atomic model. His model shows electrons traveling in orbits around an atom's nucleus. Bohr believes that an atom's chemical properties are determined by how many electrons are in its outer orbits.

1933: Milk is first fortified with Vitamin D.

1934: Citric acid is first added to food during processing.

1939: Linus Pauling publishes his work on chemical bonds.

1939: Ascorbic acid is added to processed foods to prevent browning and rancidity.

1950s: The first flavored potato chips are invented by the Irish company Tayto.

1972: High-fructose corn syrup, an artificial sugar made from corn syrup, is developed.

1974: The artificial sweetener aspartame is developed.

1976: The first microwavable frozen food products are introduced.

1976: The McCormick company identifies more of the many individual chemical flavor components of vanilla and uses that information to create its own artificial vanilla.

1986: Genetically engineered enzymes, proteins, and yeasts are developed.

1990: A team of researchers at MSG-maker Ajinomoto finds a compound in garlic that enhances sweetness, saltiness, and umami. The scientists call this effect a sixth taste: kokumi.

1996: Carbon dioxide (CO_2) is added to dairy products to improve their quality and shelf-life.

2015: The U.S. Food and Drug Administration (FDA) rules that artificial trans fats are unsafe to eat and gives foodmakers three years to eliminate them from the food supply.

2019: Researchers at Northeastern University work to identify and track more than 26,000 distinct biochemicals in food to understand better what people eat and how food affects health and disease.

THE PERIODIC TABLE OF ELEMENTS

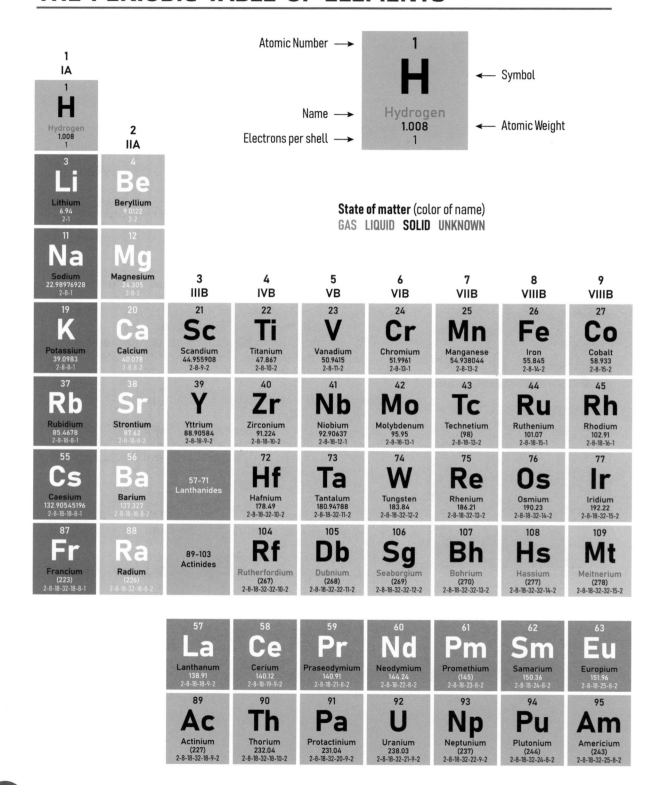

Atomic Number → 1
H ← Symbol
Name → Hydrogen
1.008 ← Atomic Weight
Electrons per shell → 1

State of matter (color of name)
GAS LIQUID **SOLID** UNKNOWN

1 IA								
1 **H** Hydrogen 1.008 1	2 IIA							
3 **Li** Lithium 6.94 2-1	4 **Be** Beryllium 9.0122 2-2							
11 **Na** Sodium 22.98976928 2-8-1	12 **Mg** Magnesium 24.305 2-8-2	3 IIIB	4 IVB	5 VB	6 VIB	7 VIIB	8 VIIIB	9 VIIIB
19 **K** Potassium 39.0983 2-8-8-1	20 **Ca** Calcium 40.078 2-8-8-2	21 **Sc** Scandium 44.955908 2-8-9-2	22 **Ti** Titanium 47.867 2-8-10-2	23 **V** Vanadium 50.9415 2-8-11-2	24 **Cr** Chromium 51.9961 2-8-13-1	25 **Mn** Manganese 54.938044 2-8-13-2	26 **Fe** Iron 55.845 2-8-14-2	27 **Co** Cobalt 58.933 2-8-15-2
37 **Rb** Rubidium 85.4678 2-8-18-8-1	38 **Sr** Strontium 87.62 2-8-18-8-2	39 **Y** Yttrium 88.90584 2-8-18-9-2	40 **Zr** Zirconium 91.224 2-8-18-10-2	41 **Nb** Niobium 92.90637 2-8-18-12-1	42 **Mo** Molybdenum 95.95 2-8-18-13-1	43 **Tc** Technetium (98) 2-8-18-13-2	44 **Ru** Ruthenium 101.07 2-8-18-15-1	45 **Rh** Rhodium 102.91 2-8-18-16-1
55 **Cs** Caesium 132.90545196 2-8-18-18-8-1	56 **Ba** Barium 137.327 2-8-18-18-8-2	57-71 Lanthanides	72 **Hf** Hafnium 178.49 2-8-18-32-10-2	73 **Ta** Tantalum 180.94788 2-8-18-32-11-2	74 **W** Tungsten 183.84 2-8-18-32-12-2	75 **Re** Rhenium 186.21 2-8-18-32-13-2	76 **Os** Osmium 190.23 2-8-18-32-14-2	77 **Ir** Iridium 192.22 2-8-18-32-15-2
87 **Fr** Francium (223) 2-8-18-32-18-8-1	88 **Ra** Radium (226) 2-8-18-32-18-8-2	89-103 Actinides	104 **Rf** Rutherfordium (267) 2-8-18-32-32-10-2	105 **Db** Dubnium (268) 2-8-18-32-32-11-2	106 **Sg** Seaborgium (269) 2-8-18-32-32-12-2	107 **Bh** Bohrium (270) 2-8-18-32-32-13-2	108 **Hs** Hassium (277) 2-8-18-32-32-14-2	109 **Mt** Meitnerium (278) 2-8-18-32-32-15-2

57 **La** Lanthanum 138.91 2-8-18-18-9-2	58 **Ce** Cerium 140.12 2-8-18-19-9-2	59 **Pr** Praseodymium 140.91 2-8-18-21-8-2	60 **Nd** Neodymium 144.24 2-8-18-22-8-2	61 **Pm** Promethium (145) 2-8-18-23-8-2	62 **Sm** Samarium 150.36 2-8-18-24-8-2	63 **Eu** Europium 151.96 2-8-18-25-8-2
89 **Ac** Actinium (227) 2-8-18-32-18-9-2	90 **Th** Thorium 232.04 2-8-18-32-18-10-2	91 **Pa** Protactinium 231.04 2-8-18-32-20-9-2	92 **U** Uranium 238.03 2-8-18-32-21-9-2	93 **Np** Neptunium (237) 2-8-18-32-22-9-2	94 **Pu** Plutonium (244) 2-8-18-32-24-8-2	95 **Am** Americium (243) 2-8-18-32-25-8-2

THE PERIODIC TABLE OF ELEMENTS

Subcategory in the metal-metalloid-nonmetal trend (color of background)

- Alkali metals
- Alkaline earth metals
- Transition metals
- Lanthanides
- Actinides
- Post-transition metals
- Metalloids
- Reactive nonmetals
- Noble gases
- Unknown chemical properties

18 VIIIA
2 **He** Helium 4.0026 2

13 IIIA	14 IVA	15 VA	16 VIA	17 VIIA
5 **B** Boron 10.81 2-3	6 **C** Carbon 12.011 2-4	7 **N** Nitrogen 14.007 2-5	8 **O** Oxygen 15.999 2-6	9 **F** Fluorine 18.998 2-7	10 **Ne** Neon 20.180 2-8

10 VIIIB	11 IB	12 IIB	13 **Al** Aluminium 26.982 2-8-3	14 **Si** Silicon 28.085 2-8-4	15 **P** Phosphorus 30.974 2-8-5	16 **S** Sulfur 32.06 2-8-6	17 **Cl** Chlorine 35.45 2-8-7	18 **Ar** Argon 39.948 2-8-8
28 **Ni** Nickel 58.693 2-8-16-2	29 **Cu** Copper 63.546 2-8-18-1	30 **Zn** Zinc 65.38 2-8-18-2	31 **Ga** Gallium 69.723 2-8-18-3	32 **Ge** Germanium 72.630 2-8-18-4	33 **As** Arsenic 74.922 2-8-18-5	34 **Se** Selenium 78.971 2-8-18-6	35 **Br** Bromine 79.904 2-8-18-7	36 **Kr** Krypton 83.798 2-8-18-8
46 **Pd** Palladium 106.42 2-8-18-18	47 **Ag** Silver 107.87 2-8-18-18-1	48 **Cd** Cadmium 112.41 2-8-18-18-2	49 **In** Indium 114.82 2-8-18-18-3	50 **Sn** Tin 118.71 2-8-18-18-4	51 **Sb** Antimony 121.76 2-8-18-18-5	52 **Te** Tellurium 127.60 2-8-18-18-6	53 **I** Iodine 126.90 2-8-18-18-7	54 **Xe** Xenon 131.29 2-8-18-18-8
78 **Pt** Platinum 195.08 2-8-18-32-17-1	79 **Au** Gold 196.97 2-8-18-32-18-1	80 **Hg** Mercury 200.59 2-8-18-32-18-2	81 **Tl** Thallium 204.38 2-8-18-32-18-3	82 **Pb** Lead 207.2 2-8-18-32-18-4	83 **Bi** Bismuth 208.98 2-8-18-32-18-5	84 **Po** Polonium (209) 2-8-18-32-18-6	85 **At** Astatine (210) 2-8-18-32-18-7	86 **Rn** Radon (222) 2-8-18-32-18-8
110 **Ds** Darmstadtium (281) 2-8-18-32-32-17-1	111 **Rg** Roentgenium (282) 2-8-18-32-32-17-2	112 **Cn** Copernicium (285) 2-8-18-32-32-18-2	113 **Nh** Nihonium (286) 2-8-18-32-32-18-3	114 **Fl** Flerovium (289) 2-8-18-32-32-18-4	115 **Mc** Moscovium (290) 2-8-18-32-32-18-5	116 **Lv** Livermorium (293) 2-8-18-32-32-18-6	117 **Ts** Tennessine (294) 2-8-18-32-32-18-7	118 **Og** Oganesson (294) 2-8-18-32-32-18-8

64 **Gd** Gadolinium 157.25 2-8-18-25-9-2	65 **Tb** Terbium 158.93 2-8-18-27-8-2	66 **Dy** Dysprosium 162.50 2-8-18-28-8-2	67 **Ho** Holmiun 164.93 2-8-18-29-8-2	68 **Er** Erbium 167.26 2-8-18-30-8-2	69 **Tm** Thulium 168.93 2-8-18-31-8-2	70 **Yb** Ytterbium 173.05 2-8-18-32-8-2	71 **Lu** Lutetium 174.97 2-8-18-32-9-2
96 **Cm** Curium (247) 2-8-18-32-25-9-2	97 **Bk** Berkelium (247) 2-8-18-32-27-8-2	98 **Cf** Californium (251) 2-8-18-32-28-8-2	99 **Es** Einsteinium (252) 2-8-18-32-29-8-2	100 **Fm** Fermium (257) 2-8-18-32-30-8-2	101 **Md** Mendelevium (258) 2-8-18-32-31-8-2	102 **No** Nobelium (259) 2-8-18-32-32-8-2	103 **Lr** Lawrencium (266) 2-8-18-32-32-8-3

Introduction
A Tasty Experiment

What is the connection between chemistry and food?

Chemistry is the study of matter, which means we encounter chemistry in every part of our lives! That's especially true in the kitchen, where chemistry dictates how food tastes, how quickly it goes bad, and what happens when heat or cold is applied to it.

How do ingredients combine to create flavorful casseroles, soups, and baked goods? What happens when you add heat to a piece of raw meat? Have you ever wondered why cooking food changes the way it tastes and feels? All of these questions can be explained by science!

At its most basic level, food is a substance like any other substance studied in science. Food is made up of atoms and molecules that follow the rules of chemistry and physics. By learning how food's molecules interact, react, and change, we begin to understand the science of food and cooking.

CHEMISTRY AND FOOD

Everything you taste, smell, and touch involves chemistry. Chemistry is the reason food tastes the way it does. Chemistry also explains what happens to food during cooking. Every time you step into the kitchen, you use chemistry.

Chemistry is in action when you simmer, boil, bake, freeze, and combine food. By learning chemistry's basic concepts and how they relate to food, we can better understand what makes our next meal so delicious.

Chemistry is the study of matter and the changes it undergoes. Matter is anything that has mass and takes up space. Everything around you, including your own body, is made of matter. Your computer is made of matter. The air you breathe, the water you drink, and the food you eat are made of matter. Fruits, vegetables, meats, cheeses, and breads are all made of matter.

Because food is simply a type of matter, chemistry's basic concepts can help us understand what food is and how it can be transformed. Let's start at the most basic level.

Food, like all matter, is governed by the rules of chemistry. Food chemistry is a branch of science that studies the substances that make up food, the chemical processes that food undergoes, and how different foods can be combined or changed to make new foods.

ATOMS: MATTER'S BASIC BUILDING BLOCKS

Like all matter, food is made up of tiny building blocks called atoms. Understanding atoms and how they work is the core of chemistry.

Atoms are made of three basic parts—protons, neutrons, and electrons. Each part of an atom has a positive, negative, or neutral electrical charge. The atom's center, called its nucleus, holds its protons and neutrons. Protons are small particles with positive electrical charges (+). Neutrons are small particles with no electrical charge.

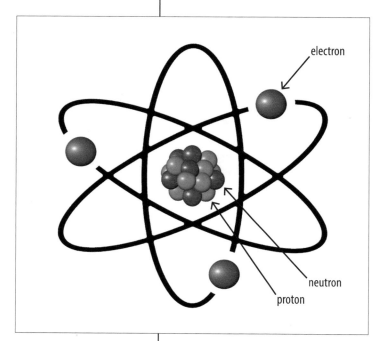

electron

neutron

proton

The number of protons in an atom determines what type of element that atom makes up.

For example, an atom with six protons makes an element called carbon, while an atom with 20 protons makes an element called calcium.

Neutrons act as stabilizers. Because protons have the same positive charge, they repel each other, just as the same ends of a magnet repel each other. Neutrons keep the protons together and stabilize the nucleus.

Electrons are small, negatively charged particles that stay outside an atom's nucleus. The negative charge of an electron attracts the positive charge of a proton, just as the opposite ends of a magnet attract each other.

This attraction between the positive protons and the negative electrons is an important force that holds the atom together.

Electrons are always moving. However, each electron is limited to moving in a specific area, called a shell. Within their assigned shells, electrons constantly spin. They move up, down, and sideways.

In an atom, the positive charge of one proton cancels out the negative charge of one electron. Therefore, if the atom has an equal number of protons and electrons, it will be neutral with no electrical charge. Yet, because electrons are always moving around, they sometimes move from one atom to another.

When an atom has more protons than electrons, it has an overall positive charge. When it has more electrons than protons, the atom has a negative charge. An atom that gains or loses an electron and has a positive or negative charge is called an ion.

An atom in the element thorium. Each electron has to stay in its assigned shell.

Elements are made entirely from one type of atom. Other types of matter are made from different combinations of atoms. Let's take a look at how these combinations happen!

FORMING MOLECULES WITH CHEMICAL BONDS

When two or more elements bond together, they form a compound. If the atoms are held together by sharing electrons, called covalent bonds, they form molecules. Molecules are held together by chemical bonds. A chemical bond isn't something you can touch, such as a piece of tape. It's a force that draws atoms together, like a magnet.

Some bonds are strong and stable, while others are weak. Although there are different types of chemical bonds, they all occur when atoms share or trade their electrons. There are two main types of chemical bonds: ionic bonds and covalent bonds. In an ionic bond, one atom captures the electron of another, which forms a strong bond that holds the two atoms together. Atoms with ionic bonds are called crystals.

Do you like salt on your steak or potato? Salt has the chemical formula NaCl. This means it is made of sodium (Na) and chlorine (Cl) atoms held together with ionic bonds.

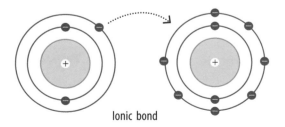

Ionic bond

What about sugar in your tea? A covalent bond occurs when two atoms, each with an extra electron, share the pair of electrons. Table sugar is a combination of carbon (C), oxygen (O), and hydrogen (H) atoms bonded together by covalent bonds. Its formula $C_{12}H_{22}O_{11}$ tells us that a sucrose, or sugar, molecule is made of 12 carbon atoms, 22 hydrogen atoms, and 11 oxygen atoms. Covalent bonds are usually strong and stable when at room temperature.

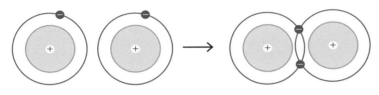

Covalent bond

MIXTURES, SOLUTIONS, COMPOUNDS, AND MORE

A pure substance has only one type of molecule. White sugar, which is also known as sucrose, is made of only sucrose molecules. Most substances are not pure, however. Instead, they are a combination of many different molecules. These combinations can be mixtures or solutions.

In a mixture, individual molecules do not chemically change or bond when they are mixed together. Have you ever poured two different kinds of candy into a bowl? The candies mix together, but each individual piece remains the same as it was before it was mixed.

Atoms form chemical bonds because they become more stable when bonded together. Electric forces attract nearby atoms to each other and cause them to stick together.

Mixtures can be separated by physical forces. Grinding, boiling, distillation, and filtering are all physical ways to separate mixtures. For example, when you boil salt water, the water evaporates into the air while the salt remains behind.

In a solution, one material, called a solute, completely dissolves in another substance, called a solvent. The molecules are mixed and evenly distributed. Sugar water is an example of a solution. Solid sugar crystals dissolve and spread evenly throughout the water. The amount of sugar in the water is the same at the top and bottom of the glass.

A solution can also be a gas dissolved in liquid. In soda and seltzer, molecules of carbon dioxide gas are dissolved in liquid water.

Other times, two or more elements can chemically combine to form a compound. A compound is a substance made of two or more elements in specific ratios. It can be broken into simpler pieces—its individual elements. They are homogenous materials, which means that they are the same all the way through and have a uniform composition.

There are millions of different compounds. Distilled water is a pure compound, as it contains only water molecules (H_2O).

CHEMICAL REACTIONS

Sometimes, when two or more substances combine, they form a completely new substance. When this occurs, it's a chemical reaction!

Chemical reactions are an important part of cooking. They allow chefs to create a meal that's delicious and very different from their basic ingredients. Have you ever made toast? That's a chemical reaction!

A chemical reaction is more than dissolving a substance in a solution, and it's more than a substance changing states from a solid to a liquid. In these cases, a substance's physical characteristics change, but not the substance itself. Water, ice, and steam all still have the chemical formula: H_2O. No new substances are formed.

But in a chemical reaction, a chemical change occurs and a new substance is created. Several clues show us a chemical reaction has occurred. Chemical reactions can produce a gas or they can form a precipitate, which is a solid substance created when two liquids combine and cause a chemical reaction.

A change in temperature that occurs without heat being added or taken away is another clue that a chemical reaction took place. New odors or colors are also signs of a chemical reaction.

Chemical bonds and compounds are why bacon smells so good!

Take a look at this video.

reactions
bacon

Fresh-baked bread is the result of a chemical reaction.

MATTER'S CHANGING STATES

All around us, matter exists in three different states, called phases. Matter can be solid, liquid, or gas. It can also change from one state to another.

> *A liquid whose molecules are strongly attracted to each other will evaporate more slowly than a liquid whose molecules are held together by a weaker attraction.*

Have you ever seen an ice cube melt? That's an example of matter in a solid form (ice) changing to a liquid form (water). When that puddle of water evaporates on a hot day, it changes form once again—this time from a liquid to a gas.

What's going on in matter to make it change states? Matter changes state when its molecules either gain or lose energy. This causes the force of attraction between the molecules to weaken or strengthen. Molecules in a solid object are tightly packed together and locked into place by strong attraction. This gives a solid object its shape and volume.

When a solid is heated, the molecules increase their movement. This motion creates enough kinetic energy, or the energy of motion, to overcome the attractions holding the molecules in place. The molecules are able to move more freely. When this occurs, the solid object changes state and melts and becomes a liquid.

The temperature at which a solid substance melts is called its melting point. Different substances have different melting points. The temperature at which a substance melts is determined by the strength of the forces of attraction among its atoms or molecules.

The stronger the intermolecular forces at work, the more energy and **higher temperature is needed to release the bonds so the substance** can shift from a solid to a liquid.

In a liquid, molecules constantly move and bump into each other. The molecules are loosely attracted. Even though they are not locked in place, the attraction between molecules is strong enough to hold them close to each other.

When a molecule in a liquid has enough energy to overcome the forces holding onto the other molecules, it escapes into the air as a gas. This process is called evaporation.

When you boil a liquid on a stove, heat energy is transferred to the liquid. The liquid's molecules move more and increase their kinetic energy, or energy of motion. The temperature of the liquid increases and more molecules escape into the air as a gas. When a liquid reaches its boiling point, the molecules spread out and form bubbles.

The molecules in a gas are moving so fast and with such a high kinetic energy that they can break away from each other's attraction completely and move freely in the air.

Many food molecules cannot change phase when heated. Instead, they undergo a chemical reaction and form entirely different molecules. For example, solid sugar will melt into a liquid when heated. However, it will not evaporate into a gas as water does. Instead, the liquid sugar breaks apart and forms new compounds in a process called caramelization.

ELEMENTS

An element is a substance that is made up of only one type of atom. It cannot be broken down into a simpler substance. Some elements, such as carbon (C), have been known for thousands of years. Others, such as moscovium (Mc), have been discovered recently. Scientists identify elements by the number of protons found in the nucleus of its atom. For example, a carbon atom has six protons, while an oxygen atom has eight protons.

Applying heat to sugar makes a crisp caramel top on this crème brûlée dessert!

All known elements are organized on a chart called the periodic table of elements. You can find the periodic table in the front pages of this book. Each element on the periodic table is located in a specific square based on its atomic structure and characteristics. Each square displays certain information about that element, including its name, symbol, atomic number, and atomic mass.

ENERGY AND HEAT

Energy and heat are very important parts of cooking, and they're very important parts of chemistry! The atoms and molecules of matter are always moving, even though you cannot see their motion with the naked eye.

These tiny moving particles have energy called kinetic energy, also known as the energy of motion.

When an atom or molecule moves faster, it has more kinetic energy than when it moves slowly. Temperature is a measure of a substance's average kinetic energy. The hotter a food is, the faster its molecules are moving and bumping into each other.

Heat adds energy to a substance. Cooking food on a hot stove transfers heat energy to the food. In turn, the food's atoms and molecules move faster and have more kinetic energy. Its temperature rises.

As a food's molecules move faster, their movement and collisions can break the chemical bonds holding them together. This frees some atoms to attach to other atoms in new molecules. In this way, heat can lead to chemical reactions in food and create new substances.

FOOD AND ITS CHEMISTRY

While a chef views cooking as mixing different ingredients to create a delicious meal, food scientists view cooking as combining different food molecules to create chemical reactions that form a new food product.

They study the chemical properties of food, how food molecules combine, and what reactions occur.

Food scientists also use the principles of chemistry and other sciences to develop new ways to use and combine ingredients. They use science to improve food's flavor, nutrition, and freshness.

In this book, you'll explore the science and chemistry behind the food you love to eat. We'll look at food ingredients and explore their molecular components. We'll study how combining ingredients and using different cooking methods creates chemical reactions that result in delicious and mouthwatering dishes.

We'll investigate the science of nutrition and learn what makes different foods healthy. Finally, we'll learn about how taste and smell combine to create flavor in food and why texture is important.

Let's get cooking!

So far, scientists have discovered 118 elements. These 118 elements combine to make millions of different substances. In the future, scientists may discover even more elements.

KEY QUESTIONS

- **What effect does heat have on different kinds of food?**

- **How do you think cold might affect food?**

- **When you think of yummy food, are you thinking about flavor or texture? Or both?**

- **Why is chemistry part of lots of different sciences?**

TEXT TO WORLD

What other chemical reactions are part of your everyday life?

CHEMICAL OR PHYSICAL?

In the kitchen, chefs combine and alter food ingredients to create a finished dish. Some of these changes are physical—the food changes form, shape, and size—but the molecules that make up the food do not change. Other changes in food are chemical. When food undergoes a chemical reaction, a new substance is created. During a chemical change, bonds within molecules are created or destroyed. In this activity, you will classify different changes food undergoes during cooking as either physical or chemical.

CAUTION: Always ask an adult to help with cooking!

VOCAB LAB 📖

Write down what you think each word means. What root words can you find to help you? What does the context of the word tell you?

atom, bond, chemical reaction, compound, element, kinetic energy, mixture, molecule, solution, and **temperature**.

Compare your definitions with those of your friends or classmates. Did you all come up with the same meanings? Turn to the text and glossary if you need help.

- **Choose a few of the "recipes" below.**

  - Prepare a mixed green salad with chopped vegetables, shredded cheese, and sliced almonds.

  - Make a fruit smoothie by blending fruit, ice, and juice.

  - Make popsicles by placing fruit juice into popsicle forms and placing in the freezer.

  - Make pancakes by preparing batter and frying on a griddle.

  - Sauté onions in butter on a stovetop.

  - Cut an apple into slices and let it sit for a period of time.

- **Did a physical or chemical change occur?** Is there a new odor or color? Did you hear any kind of sound from the ingredients? These can be signs of a chemical change.

- **Explain your reasoning for your conclusions.** Record your observations in your science journal.

To investigate more, pick another recipe to watch for physical and chemical changes. What physical changes to food ingredients do you observe? What chemical changes? Is there any evidence of a chemical change?

Chapter 1

The Chemicals in Our Food

Why are there so many chemicals in food?

Chemicals are the foundation of everything, including food! Different types of chemicals, both natural and artificial, make up everything we eat, and the combinations of these chemicals decide the flavor, texture, behavior, and nutritional value of our food.

Pizza, carrots, tortilla chips, strawberry pie—everything you eat is made of chemicals! Many chemicals in food occur naturally, such as water, lipids, carbohydrates, and proteins. Other chemicals in food are created artificially. Together, molecules are the building blocks that combine in specific ways to create your favorite foods. The combination of molecules in food affects the way it tastes, looks, and feels. It's the molecules in your favorite meatball sandwich that make it taste so good!

Most foods are made of four basic types of molecules: water, lipids, carbohydrates, and proteins. These molecules combine in different ratios and combinations to create the food we eat. The properties of a food's molecules change how it tastes, looks, and feels. They also influence what happens to food during cooking.

Let's take a closer look!

WATER, WATER, EVERYWHERE

Water is a major part of nearly all foods. Fruits and vegetables are about 95 percent water molecules, while raw meat is about 75 percent water. To understand how water molecules behave in food and cooking, we need to look at their properties.

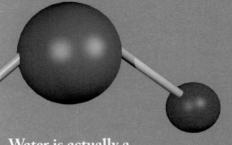

A water molecule is a polar molecule. This means that it has a positively charged end and a negatively charged end. The molecule's three atoms share electrons through covalent bonds. However, the oxygen atom pulls more strongly on those shared electrons. This strong pull brings the shared electrons closer to the oxygen end of the molecule. Because electrons have a negative charge, this gives the molecule's oxygen end a slight negative charge. As a result, the molecule's hydrogen ends have a slight positive charge.

Opposite charges attract each other. When two water molecules are near each other, the negative end of one is attracted to the positive end of the other. This force of attraction between two water molecules is fairly strong compared to most forces between molecules.

Since the hydrogen ends of one molecule attract the oxygen end of another molecule, this attractive force is called a hydrogen bond. It is much weaker than the covalent bonds between hydrogen and oxygen atoms inside the molecule itself, yet these hydrogen bonds help explain how water molecules behave in food and cooking. Remember, water makes up a large percentage of all food. How water acts and reacts will have a major influence on what happens to the food when it's baked, boiled, fried, or barbecued!

Water is actually a very simple molecule. A water molecule (H_2O) is made of just three atoms: two hydrogen atoms (H) and one oxygen atom (O). Despite its simplicity, water has a very important role in food and cooking.

FLOATING FUN

Water in its frozen form is unique.

Generally, solid matter is more dense than liquid matter, because its atoms and molecules are packed together more closely—that's why rocks sink. However, in frozen water, the molecules are organized to evenly distribute their hydrogen bonds. As a result, solid ice actually has more space between its molecules than liquid water. That's why ice cubes float in your glass of lemonade. It's also why a container of leftover soup that is filled to the brim will burst in the freezer. As the soup freezes, the water in it expands and takes up more space!

Water's hydrogen bonds affect how the molecules absorb and transmit heat. When water freezes into solid ice, its molecules pack together in organized crystals. As ice warms, its molecules move more, generate more kinetic energy, and break some of the hydrogen bonds. That's when the ice melts into liquid water.

As the temperature increases, the water molecules move even faster and generate even more kinetic energy. Some molecules break free of their hydrogen bonds completely and escape as water vapor into the air.

Water's hydrogen bonds also make liquid water slow to heat. When you put a pot of water on the stove, the heat energy must first break the hydrogen bonds before water's molecules can

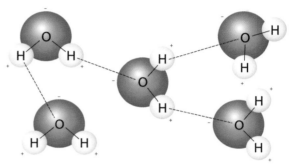

Water molecules bond together through hydrogen bonds

move faster. This allows water to absorb a lot of heat without itself becoming hot. A covered pan of water will take more than twice as long as a pan of oil to heat to the same temperature.

Water is also considered a universal solvent. A solvent is a liquid in which a substance—called a solute—dissolves. Almost everything dissolves in water, from sugar and salt to ground coffee beans. How does this work? In food, both carbohydrate and protein molecules have polar areas. Water molecules are attracted to these polar areas and surround them. This separates the solute's molecules from each other and those molecules spread out and dissolve in water.

LIPIDS: FATS AND OILS

Lipids are a large family of food molecules commonly known as fats and oils. Fats and oils give food flavor and a smooth consistency. They tenderize some foods and help cook others.

Fats are important for the body and are a major source of energy. They are necessary for some body processes, such as blood clotting and muscle movement. Fats also help the body absorb certain vitamins and minerals. In addition, fats are used to build cell membranes and the sheaths that surround nerves.

All lipid molecules have a similar chemical structure: a chain of carbon (C) atoms bonded to some hydrogen (H) atoms. In different types of lipid molecules, the length and shape of the carbon chain and the number of hydrogen atoms connected to the carbon atoms vary.

Because of their similar structures, all lipids share a characteristic—they don't mix well with water. Have you ever seen Italian salad dressing separate in the bottle? This happens because the covalent bonds between the lipid's carbon and hydrogen atoms are nonpolar, so the two atoms pull equally on their shared electrons. When nonpolar lipids mix with polar water molecules, the water molecules cluster together while the lipid molecules cluster with themselves. That's why when you combine oil and water, the oil forms large, visible blobs in the water.

Try it yourself! With an adult's permission, pour a little bit of cooking oil into a glass of water. Stir it up with a fork. What happens? What does the mixture look like after a minute has passed?

When oil is poured into water, the two substances don't mix!

THE SKINNY ON FATS

All fats are not created equal. Some are considered healthy, while others are not. What's the difference?

Trans fats are considered the worst type of fat in food. They are a byproduct of a process called hydrogenation, which turns healthy oils into solids so that they do not become rancid. Trans fats are unhealthy because they increase the amount of a harmful substance called LDL cholesterol in your blood, which can build up as plaque on the inside of blood vessels. As time passes, this causes the blood vessels to narrow, which increases your risk of heart disease and stroke.

Trans fats also cause inflammation in the body, which has been linked to heart disease, stroke, diabetes, and other chronic diseases. Today, trans fats are banned in the United States and in many other countries.

Saturated fat is another type of fat that is generally solid at room temperature. Saturated fat is found in red meat, whole milk, whole milk dairy foods, cheese, coconut oil, and many processed baked goods and other foods. The chain of carbon atoms in saturated fat is connected by single bonds only. The chain is "saturated" with hydrogen atoms.

It's healthy to limit the amount of saturated fats you eat.

Eating a lot of saturated fats is considered unhealthy bacause too much can lead to an increase in that harmful LDL cholesterol in the body. This can lead to narrowing and blockages in the arteries in the body.

Unlike saturated fat, unsaturated fat has one or more double bonds connecting their carbon chains. Unsaturated fat is mainly found in vegetables, nuts, seeds, and fish—it is liquid at room temperature. This type of fat is considered healthy, essential fat. The body needs it for normal body functions, such as building cell membranes and blood clotting.

Have you ever let a stick of butter sit out on the counter for a few hours? What happens? It might soften over time, but it never melts. Fats have a wide range of melting points, which is the temperature at which a solid melts into a liquid. As the temperature increases, the fat molecules melt at different points. They slowly weaken the solid structure, which makes the butter softer.

This is important in baking because fats are crucial for making pastries and cakes!

If you place the butter in a pan on the stove and continue to increase the temperature, it eventually melts into liquid form. Fat's high melting point is a result of the large size of the fat molecules.

Fat's long carbon chains form weak bonds with each other. But because they can form so many bonds along both long chains, it takes more heat energy to break them all apart from each other. The longer the fat's chain of atoms, the higher its melting point will be. Keep raising the temperature, and the melted fat will eventually transform from a liquid into a gas. This occurs only at a very high temperature, much hotter than water's boiling point.

OMEGA-3 FATTY ACIDS

Omega-3 fatty acids are a type of healthy, unsaturated fat. Omega-3 fatty acids are essential fats, which means the body does not make them—you must get them from food. Foods rich in omega-3 fatty acids include fatty fish such as salmon and mackerel, vegetable oils, walnuts, flax seeds, flaxseed oil, and leafy vegetables. Studies have linked a diet rich in omega-3 fatty acids to several health benefits. They may help prevent heart disease and stroke. They may also help control diseases such as lupus, eczema, and rheumatoid arthritis. These fatty acids might even protect the body from some cancers and other conditions.

CARBOHYDRATES: ENERGY STORES

Carbohydrates are a group of molecules produced by plants and animals to store chemical energy. They are built from carbon (C), oxygen (O), and hydrogen (H) atoms.

Sugars are some of the most common carbohydrates. Sugar molecules come **in many different types, and each type has a different arrangement** and number of carbon atoms.

Sugars are essential to the human body. Two sugars, ribose and deoxyribose, are essential pieces of deoxyribonucleic acid (DNA) and ribonucleic acid (RNA), which are the molecules that carry the genetic code in every cell in the body. Glucose is another type of sugar that provides energy for the body's cells to function and grow.

Another common carbohydrate in food is starch. Potatoes, rice, and pasta are all foods high in starch. Plants use starches to store their supplies of sugar. Starch consists of a chain of glucose sugar molecules. Plants produce two forms of starch: a long, straight chain of glucose molecules called amylose and a highly branched chain called amylopectin. Each form can hold thousands of glucose molecules.

FOOD FACT

Sugars are so important for the body's functioning that humans have a special taste sense designed to detect them. Eating foods with sugar triggers a sense of pleasure in the body. That's why humans like to eat sweet foods such as fruits, candies, and cakes.

During cooking, starch in the form of tiny granules bonds to water and other liquids. As the starch absorbs liquid, the liquid thickens. As the temperature rises, the liquid bonds more readily to the starch. The starch swells and becomes thicker and stickier. This is what happens when you boil dried pasta. The starch in the pasta absorbs water and swells, which causes the dry pasta to become soft and slightly sticky.

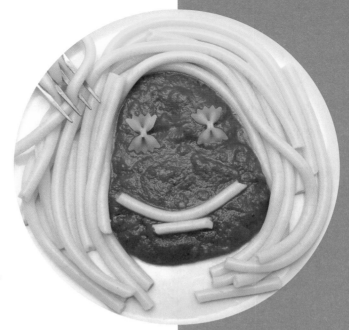

PROTEINS: HELPING THE BODY FUNCTION

Proteins are another major type of molecule in food. Proteins are at the center of an organism's activity, growth, and movement. They assemble all molecules in a cell and move molecules from one part of a cell to another. Unlike other major food molecules—water, fats, and carbohydrates, which are generally stable—proteins are quick to change. When exposed to heat, acid, salt, or air, the behavior of protein molecules can change dramatically.

Proteins are made from many smaller molecules called amino acids. Currently, there are 23 known amino acids. In cooking, amino acids play an important role. Many amino acids have their own taste and contribute flavor to food. Most are either sweet or bitter, while a few taste savory. Amino acids that contain sulfur molecules have an eggy, meaty flavor when heated and broken down.

During cooking, changes to protein molecules result in new substances and consistencies in food. Think of eggs, which are high in protein. How does adding heat to an egg change it? How many different kinds of cooked eggs can you think of?

Watch this video to see why some hard-boiled egg yolks turn green.

ⓟ
overcooked egg chemistry

PROTEIN PLUS WATER

In most foods and organisms, protein molecules are surrounded by water. All proteins are able to form hydrogen bonds, so they can absorb and hold some water molecules. How the protein does this depends on the type of protein and its structure. Protein molecules can hold water molecules inside the protein folds, along the backbone, or on the side groups sticking out from the chain's backbone. Whether or not a protein dissolves in water depends on the strength of the bonds between the protein molecules.

Amino acids are linked in a long chain to form a variety of protein molecules. The protein molecule twists and forms a helix, or spiral. Because the chain is so long, the protein often bends and folds. This folding and bonding gives each protein molecule its three-dimensional shape and allows it to perform its intended job.

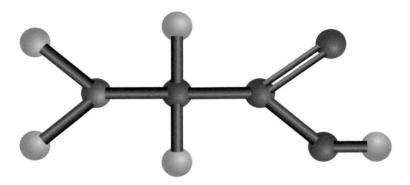

A glycine amino acid structure

ENZYME ACTION

Enzymes are a specific type of protein that act as catalysts. Catalysts cause chemical change and speed the rate of chemical reactions. Some enzymes build or change molecules. Other enzymes break down molecules.

In the human body, digestive enzymes break down the proteins in food into individual amino acids. When cooking, enzymes can change the color, texture, taste, or nutritional value of food. Enzymes are what cause a cut apple to turn brown and vegetables to turn mushy. Bacterial enzymes break down and spoil food. That's what's at work on the forgotten pineapple in the back of your fridge!

FOOD FACT

Amino acids are molecules made up of about 10 to 40 atoms, mainly carbon, hydrogen, oxygen, and nitrogen.

Cooking can affect enzyme action. When enzymes are heated, they become more active. Once they reach a certain temperature, they unfold and become inactive.

Sometimes, chefs want enzymes to act, for example, to help tenderize a tough piece of meat. In this case, a slow, gradual heating process to cook the meat allows more time for enzyme action. Other times, a chef wants to prevent enzyme action. In this situation, heating the food as quickly as possible limits the time during which the enzymes can act.

VITAMINS AND MINERALS

The food we eat also contains small amounts of vitamins and minerals. Vitamins are organic compounds. This means they contain at least one carbon atom, which is needed for life. The human body does not produce enough vitamins to sustain life, so humans get most of the vitamins they need from food. Currently, we know of 13 essential vitamins. In addition to A, C, D, E, and K, there are eight B vitamins: B1 (thiamine), B2 (riboflavin), B3 (niacin), B5 (pantothenic acid), B6 (pyroxidine), B7 (biotin), B9 (folate), and B12 (cobalamin).

Vitamins are either fat-soluble, which means they dissolve in fats, or water-soluble, which means they dissolve in water. The fat-soluble vitamins—A, D, E, and K—are stored in the body's fatty tissues and liver. The body can store these vitamins for days and even months. They are absorbed through the body's intestinal tract.

Water-soluble vitamins, including C and the B vitamins, cannot be stored in the body for a long time. These need to be replaced frequently.

PINEAPPLE GELATIN

Did you know that adding fresh pineapple to gelatin prevents it from gelling? Pineapples contains two enzymes that digest proteins. Gelatins get their gel-like structure when links form between chains of collagen, a type of protein. When pineapple is added to the gelatin, the enzymes prevent the collagen chains from linking. Canned pineapple is heated during the canning process, which inactivates its enzymes. With canned pineapple, the gelatin sets in a beautiful gel dessert.

TOXIC COMPOUNDS

Sometimes, bacteria and molds produce toxic compounds in food. A tiny amount of toxic compounds doesn't usually hurt you, but some compounds can cause sickness or even death. Botulism is a type of food poisoning that you can get from eating food that contains the toxin of the bacteria *Clostridium botulinum*. Botulinum toxin is destroyed at 185 degrees Fahrenheit (85 degrees Celsius), but botulism spores are not killed until they reach temperatures greater than 250 degrees Fahrenheit (121 degrees Celsius). Spores can produce toxin in cooked and canned foods. That's why many home canned goods have to be processed at higher temperatures in a pressure canner.

Each vitamin has a job in the human body. For example, vitamin A protects against eye disorders, such as night-blindness. We get vitamin A from several foods—liver, carrots, broccoli, sweet potatoes, butter, kale, spinach, eggs, cantaloupe, and milk, to name a few. Vitamin D helps strengthen the body's bones and teeth. Foods that provide vitamin D include fatty fish, eggs, mushrooms, and liver.

Most nutritionists recommend that we get most of our vitamins by eating a balanced variety of healthy foods, with lots of fruits and vegetables. In some cases, people who cannot get enough of certain vitamins through their foods might take vitamin supplements.

The human body also needs essential minerals to develop and **function properly. Minerals are inorganic elements found** on Earth and in food.

THE CHEMISTRY OF FOOD I CHAPTER ONE

The body uses minerals for many things, from sending nerve impulses to building strong bones. Some minerals help make hormones and keep the heart beating normally.

There are two groups of minerals: macro minerals and trace minerals. The body needs greater amounts of macro minerals to function. These include calcium, phosphorus, magnesium, sodium, potassium, chloride, and sulfur. The body needs only a little bit of trace minerals. Trace minerals include iron, manganese, copper, iodine, zinc, cobalt, fluoride, and selenium.

Like vitamins, each mineral has a specific purpose in the body. For example, iron is necessary to form hemoglobin, which is the part of the body's red blood cells that carries oxygen throughout the body. Foods that are good sources of iron include leafy green vegetables, red meat, tuna, salmon, eggs, beans, and whole grains.

OTHER CHEMICALS IN FOOD

Sometimes, food processors and packagers add preservatives and other additives to make food stay fresher, taste better, and look more appealing. For centuries, people have added preservatives to slow spoilage from mold, yeast, botulism, and other microorganisms.

Some preservatives are natural. People have long used salt to preserve meat and fish. They have added sugar to preserve canned foods and vinegar to pickle vegetables.

Watch this video to learn more about the six essential nutrients you get from food and why your body needs them.

ⓟ
how the six basic nutrients affect your body

KEY QUESTIONS

- **Why does pasta get soft when it's cooked?**
- **What are some ways the body is affected by fats?**
- **What role do carbohydrates play in the body? Proteins?**

Fats and oils have different melting points, so fats are solid at room temperature while oils are liquid. Basically, oils are liquid fats.

TEXT TO WORLD

Have you ever had a craving for a certain kind of food? What do you think your body is asking for when it craves this food?

In modern times, companies often use synthetic chemicals as artificial preservatives in processed food. Preservatives bind water and makes it unavailable for microorganisms to use, which slows their growth and prevents food spoilage.

Other additives are used in food for a variety of reasons. Many milk products have traces of antibiotics in them because of treatments given to dairy cows to prevent disease. Emulsifying agents are added to liquids to help them blend better.

Anticaking agents such as calcium silicate prevent salt from clumping. Antioxidants prevent fats from becoming rancid. Gums are chemical additives that make ice creams and yogurts smoother. Artificial colorants and flavorings make food look and taste more appealing.

Even though the U.S. Food and Drug Administration (FDA) has approved the use of many preservatives and additives in food, consuming large quantities of some additives can be harmful. For example, large quantities of sodium nitrate, a preservative used in processed meats, have been linked to cancer. Sodium benzoate, a food preservative, and some artificial food colorings may increase hyperactivity in children.

From apples, broccoli, and bread to olive oil, salmon, and steak, the **food we eat is made of chemicals.**

By understanding the chemicals in food, their properties, and how they affect food's taste, chefs can better combine ingredients to create an appetizing dish.

KEEP YOUR DISTANCE: OIL AND WATER

Have you ever heard two people who don't get along described as "oil and water?" In this activity, you'll see firsthand what that means!

- **Fill a large jar partway with 1 cup of water.** Then, add a few drops of food coloring and stir to combine. What do you observe? How do you explain what is happening to the water and food coloring? Record your ideas in your science journal.

- **Add 1 cup of vegetable oil to the jar.** Put the jar lid on and tighten to seal. Carefully shake the liquid mixture for 15 to 20 seconds over a sink.

- **Place the jar on a flat surface.** What does it look like immediately after shaking? Observe the liquid in the jar for a few minutes. What happens to the oil and water? Why does this occur?

- **Next, open the jar and add 2 teaspoons of dish soap.** Tighten the lid again and shake the jar for 15 to 20 seconds. Place the jar on a flat surface and observe its contents for a few minutes. What happens after you add the dish soap to the jar? How do you explain what you are seeing?

> To investigate more, try adding a teaspoon of salt to the mixture. What do you observe? How do you explain your observations? You can repeat this experiment with other ingredients— such as sugar or baking soda. What happens?

VOCAB LAB

Write down what you think each word means. What root words can you find to help you? What does the context of the word tell you?

additive, carbohydrate, enzyme, glucose, lipid, protein, saturated fat, starch, trace mineral, trans fats, and **unsaturated fat**.

Compare your definitions with those of your friends or classmates. Did you all come up with the same meanings? Turn to the text and glossary if you need help.

WHAT FOOD ADDITIVES ARE IN YOUR KITCHEN?

Many foods in your kitchen contain additives and preservatives. An additive is included in a food to make it taste or look better. A preservative is added to a food to make it stay fresh longer. Additives and preservatives can be from a natural source or made synthetically in a laboratory. In this activity, you will investigate several foods in your kitchen and determine what additives and preservatives (if any) they contain.

- **Select five food items from your kitchen.** Without looking at the nutritional labels, predict how many additives and preservatives each has. How many do you think will be natural? Artificial?

- **For each food selected, investigate its nutritional label.**

  - What additives and/or preservatives are in this food?

  - What is the function of each additive/preservative?

  - How is it made and what is it made from?

  - Is it natural or artificial?

  - What foods is this additive/preservative typically used in?

  - Does this additive/preservative have any known possible side effects?

- **Repeat for each food selected.** Create a chart in your science journal to summarize and present what you have learned. Do any of your discoveries surprise you?

To investigate more, choose a food that is labeled "No Artificial Additives or Preservatives" and review its nutritional label. Why did the food producer make this claim on the food's label? What (if any) additives and preservatives are in this food? Do these substances make the food a healthier choice? Why or why not?

Chapter 2 ▶

Cooking: A Chemical Reaction

COOKING TRANSFORMS FOOD INTO SOMETHING NEW AND DELICIOUS, SUCH AS A ROASTED OR TOASTED MARSHMALLOW.

WHAT'S THE DIFF?

I LIKE MINE ON FIRE!

How does heat affect food?

Heat creates many different kinds of chemical reactions that result in food that is flavorful, easier to chew, and easier to digest. Heat makes food taste amazing!

Every chef is a chemist! Chemists study what matter is made of and how it reacts to other substances. In the kitchen, chefs experiment with a variety of compounds and substances. Every day, they denature proteins, crystallize compounds, mix ingredients, and experiment with acids and bases. They trigger physical and chemical reactions in the substances they work with and incorporate enzymes to speed or slow those reactions. What's a simpler way of saying all of this? Chefs cook food!

During cooking, food undergoes many different kinds of changes. Some of these changes are physical, while others are chemical. Physical changes include peeling, chopping, slicing, and pureeing. When food changes form, for example, when butter melts in a pan, that's another physical change. A physical change also occurs when you mix substances but the substances remain the same.

For example, you can mix carbon dioxide and flavored water to create soda. The two substances are mixed, but molecularly remain the same. They do not create a new substance and can be unmixed later. What happens when you leave a soda out for a few hours? The carbon dioxide escapes into the air, leaving the flat, flavored water in the glass.

Chemical changes, called chemical reactions, that happen in the kitchen create an entirely new substance. They also change the flavor, texture, and appearance of food—eggs, sugar, flour, chocolate, and butter go into an oven and come out as brownies!

A chemical reaction occurs when the bonds between the atoms or molecules in a substance such as food are broken and reform to create new compounds.

A good kitchen chemist knows how to control the physical and chemical changes in food in order to produce a delicious meal. Let's take a closer look at these changes.

ENDOTHERMIC VS. EXOTHERMIC REACTIONS

Chemical reactions occur when molecules bump into each other, triggering them to share, discard, or release atoms, which re-combine to form new molecules. In a chemical reaction, molecules react with each other and their atoms are re-arranged into new molecules.

Chemical reactions can be either exothermic or endothermic. An exothermic reaction releases heat when it occurs. An endothermic reaction absorbs heat. In cooking, many chemical reactions are endothermic, which means heat energy is needed to make the reaction happen. For example, when you scramble eggs in a pan, heat energy from the stove is transferred to the eggs and triggers chemical reactions. In this endothermic reaction, the raw eggs turn into a new substance—scrambled eggs.

Cooking transforms food into something new and delicious. Most of the time, cooks transform food by applying heat. Heat triggers physical and chemical reactions in the food's protein, fat, and carbohydrate molecules. It causes food molecules to move faster, collide harder, and react to form new molecules. The temperature used in cooking determines how food's molecules react and what chemical reactions occur.

Heating food destroys harmful bacteria and other microorganisms, making food safe to eat.

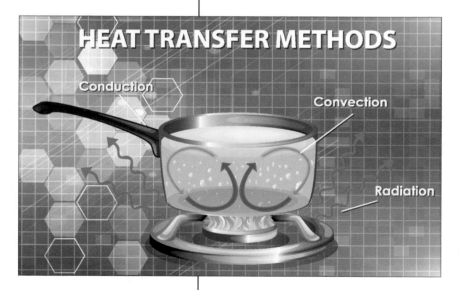

HEAT TRANSFER METHODS

Conduction

Convection

Radiation

Every time you bake cookies, broil chicken, or boil noodles, you transfer energy from a heat source to food, where it causes physical and chemical change. Heat energy in cooking is transferred in three main ways—conduction, convection, and radiation.

Let's look at how each method works to help us understand how cooking techniques affect food.

HEAT CONDUCTION

Have you ever noticed what happens if you leave a metal spoon in a cup with a hot liquid? The spoon gets hot! In fact, the longer the spoon sits in the hot liquid, the hotter the spoon becomes. This occurs because heat from the liquid is transferred to the spoon through conduction.

Heat transfer through conduction takes place when two objects are touching. When molecules in an object are heated, they move faster and vibrate. They collide with surrounding molecules.

These collisions produce and transfer heat energy from one object to another.

What happens when you turn on the burner of the stove? It gets hot, right? The burner transfers that heat energy to the bottom of a pan sitting on top of it. Then, the pan transfers the heat energy to the food it holds. Metals are good conductors of heat, which is why many cooking pots and pans are made of metals.

Conduction can also occur within a food. Have you ever noticed that when you cook a steak in a pan on the stove, the outside of the meat may be hot, while the inside is still very pink and cool? Heat travels first from the pan to cook the outside of the steak. Then, heat travels from the outside of the steak to its center.

This is done all through the process of conduction!

Most chemical reactions do not start spontaneously. For the reaction to begin, the molecules involved need to have an extra energy boost to kick off the reaction. This energy boost is called activation energy. In cooking, heating food to a certain temperature can supply the activation energy needed to start chemical reactions.

Take a look at this video to explore why heat transfer is so important in cooking.

a tasting of culinary science—heat transfer

Because the cells of most foods are not great conductors, foods usually heat up slowly. One important part of being a good cook is knowing how to heat a food at its center without overheating, or burning, its exterior. Mastering how to do this allows a chef to cook the perfect steak!

CONVECTION COOKING

Another form of heat transfer in cooking, called convection, forces molecules in the air or in a liquid to move from warmer areas to cooler areas. As molecules near a heat source become warm, they move to a cooler area. Then, the heated molecules are replaced by cooler molecules that slide in near the heat source so they can be warmed, too.

Natural convection cooking occurs when liquid at the bottom of a cooking container gets warmer and rises while the cooler, denser liquid at the top of the container sinks.

This molecule movement creates a circulating current in the container that evenly distributes heat throughout the food being cooked.

Think of a pot of water being heated to a boil on the stovetop. The water molecules closest to the bottom and sides of the pot heat first through the process of conduction. Then, convection causes the heated molecules to move away from the bottom and sides of the pot.

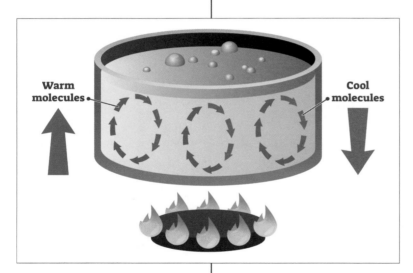

Warm molecules

Cool molecules

As the heated molecules move, they are replaced with cooler molecules. This movement transfers convection heat throughout the water. In an oven, air near the heat source rises and circulates and is replaced by cooler air. The heated air penetrates the food, which assists the cooking process.

Convection can also occur mechanically, when outside forces circulate heat. For example, a convection oven is special type of oven that uses a fan to circulate hot air over and around food. This mechanical convection circulates heat, which shortens cooking times and cooks food more evenly.

Stirring a liquid in a pot is another example of mechanical convection. The stirring action circulates molecules in the liquid, which spreads the heat energy faster and more evenly throughout the liquid.

FOOD FACT

Dark surfaces soak up radiant heat, while bright, shiny surfaces reflect it. That's why many baking recipes call for a shorter cooking time when using dark baking pans.

RADIANT HEAT METHODS

Radiant heat is different from other cooking methods—it does not require food to be in direct contact with a heat source. Instead, radiant heat uses energy emitted in electromagnetic waves. Think about how your body warms up when you stand in the summer sun. Electromagnetic waves from the sun travel through space and heat your skin.

Microwave ovens are an example of radiant heat cooking. In a microwave, short, high-frequency waves penetrate food. The waves cause the food's polar water molecules to move faster, which generates heat. The heat energy moves through the food via the process of conduction (for solids) or convection (for liquids).

In cooking, an oven's broiler is an example of radiant heat. The broiler's heating element produces electromagnetic waves. When these waves reach food in the oven, they cause the food's atoms to move faster, which generates heat. This cooks the food.

Because these microwaves can penetrate foods several inches deep, they can cook foods quickly. As we learned in the last chapter, water molecules are the biggest part of most foods, which makes microwave cooking an efficient way to heat food.

In real life, most cooking methods use a combination of several forms of heat transfer. For example, heating a pan of water on an electric stove uses all three methods. The electrical heating element radiates heat. It also transfers heat via conduction to the pan. The pan transfers heat to the water through conduction, while convection spreads heat throughout the water in the pan.

Knowing how heat transfer occurs can help a chef better understand **the science of cooking and improve their skills in the kitchen.**

A PHYSICAL CHANGE

Most food preparation involves heating food, which, as we've learned, causes change in food. Some changes, such as phase transitions, are physical.

For example, when you boil a pot of water, heat raises the water's temperature to its boiling point (212 degrees Fahrenheit or 100 degrees Celsius). At this temperature, water molecules vibrate so much they begin to break their hydrogen bonds with other water molecules. Some water molecules escape into the air as water vapor, a gas. Because water is in so many foods, this explains why cooking food too long can make it dry.

Watch this demonstration of convection!

What else could you use to see it in action?

angles acid convection

Heat can also change the physical form of fats. At room temperature, fats, such as butter, are solid. When heat is added, the solid fat melts and becomes liquid. Because you can melt fats and heat them to high temperatures, they are often used to cook foods, such as to sauté onions in melted butter.

Cooking pasta is another example of a physical change. When starches are heated, they absorb liquids in a process called gelatinization. When you boil a hard piece of dried pasta or rice in water, the pasta or rice absorbs some of the water and becomes larger and softer. In a similar way, adding flour to soups and stews can thicken them as the starch in the flour absorbs some of the liquid.

CHEMICAL CHANGE: CARAMELIZATION

Heat can also cause chemical changes in food. When a chemical reaction occurs, food molecules break apart and recombine to form different molecules. These new molecules create new flavors and new substances. Unlike phase transitions, chemical reactions in food are generally not reversible.

One of the most common chemical changes that occurs in cooking is caramelization.

Caramelization happens when sugar is cooked over low heat, which changes how the sugar looks and tastes. The chemical reaction in caramelization causes the sugar molecules to break down. The newly released chemicals form new compounds that create flavors often described as buttery and nutty. The new chemical compounds cause the food to turn a deep golden-brown color.

Phase transitions are generally reversible. For example, melted butter hardens back into a solid as it cools. Water vapor condenses into liquid water drops as it cools.

Watch a chef discuss the chemistry of gelatinization!

What kinds of foods have you eaten this week that have experienced thickening?

Culinary Institute America starch

THE MAILLARD REACTION

Another common chemical reaction in cooking is the Maillard reaction, named after Louis Camille Maillard (1878–1936), a French physician. This reaction results in many colors and flavors in cooked food.

The browning of bread into toast is the result of the Maillard reaction. When bread bakes, the outside of the bread dough is exposed to the oven's hot air. This causes chemical reactions in the outside dough, and the crust turns brown. Because the dough on the inside of the bread is not heated enough to trigger the reaction, it remains light in color.

The colors and flavors of coffee beans, chocolate, dark beers, and roasted meats are all caused by Maillard reactions.

The Maillard reaction is a chemical reaction between amino acids and simple sugars. When heated, a carbohydrate molecule and an amino acid react and form new molecules. These intermediate molecules are unstable—they move around a lot and break off from each other to form more new molecules. That's lots more reactions that form hundreds of different molecules and byproducts.

FOOD FACT

• • • • • • • • • • • • • •

While caramelization produces new flavors and colors, it does not create new vitamins or nutrients.

All these changes create a brown color and full, intense flavor in food. Maillard flavors are more intense than flavors created by caramelization. This is because the flavor compounds created in the reactions include nitrogen and sulfur atoms from amino acids, which change the taste.

Have you ever wondered why, when you cook a piece of meat, sometimes it tastes better than other times? The answer might lie in the Maillard reaction. This complex chemical reaction between sugars and amino acids in the meat produces hundreds of flavor compounds! However, the reaction depends on both time and temperature. If a chef alters either or both of these variables, different products can result.

While an expert chef is usually skilled at managing time and temperature to achieve nearly the same cooking results with every steak, a beginning cook might experience major differences in flavor and taste when cooking the same dish. Expert chefs make sure the surface of a steak is dry before searing it. If the steak is damp, the water absorbs the energy and keeps the temperature from rising quickly. This means the temperatures required for the Maillard reaction to occur may not be reached and the steak will look gray and not brown.

Plus, crowding food in a pot or pan can prevent the Maillard reaction from occurring. For example, when Portobello mushrooms are sautéed in a hot pan, they release water. If many mushrooms are crowded into the pan, they release more water, which lowers the temperature of the pan and mushrooms in it.

Maillard reactions begin at lower temperatures than caramelization. For Maillard reactions to occur, foods generally must be heated above 285 degrees Fahrenheit (140 degrees Celsius).

DRAWBACKS OF DELICIOUSNESS

Sometimes, when chemical reactions during cooking change or destroy a food's amino acids, the food's nutritional value decreases. Plus, some evidence suggests that certain products of browning reactions may be linked to cancers and DNA damage. More research is needed to better understand the long-term health effects of these changes.

This lower temperature prevents the Maillard reaction from occurring and browning the mushrooms properly. However, if the mushrooms are not crowded in the pan, the water they release evaporates more easily. The food can then heat to the proper temperature for the Maillard reaction to occur. This causes browning and the mushrooms become golden and meaty tasting.

PROTEIN DENATURATION AND COAGULATION

With foods that contain protein molecules, such as meats, eggs, and cheeses, the cooking process can change a protein's structure. The sequence of amino acids in the protein chain remains the same, but the way it folds and bonds with other parts of the chain alters. Changing a protein's shape changes its behavior.

Renaturation

Normal protein

Denatured protein

Denaturation

The process of causing a protein to lose its shape is called denaturation. Proteins can be denatured in several ways. Heat, acids, and even air bubbles can cause a protein to denature. In each situation, new chemical or physical conditions cause a protein molecule to become more agitated and break many of the attractive forces and bonds that create its folded shape. The long protein chain unfolds and more of the chain's atoms are exposed.

When long, unfolded protein molecules bump into each other, their exposed atoms are more likely to bond with each other.

This process of bonding between protein chains is called protein coagulation. As they bond, the unfolded protein molecules move closer together. In cooking, this causes food to become thicker and denser.

Often, there are water molecules in small pockets between the protein chains. This combination of denatured proteins and water molecules can create a delicious and delicate custard or a beautifully cooked piece of fish.

If denaturation and coagulation continue for too long, however, the protein molecules bond together more and more tightly. They squeeze the water molecules out from between the protein molecules. This causes the custard to become denser and the fish to become tough and dry.

Have you ever cooked eggs? When you crack an egg into a skillet, the egg white is a clear liquid. As heat is applied, the egg white turns solid and opaque white in color. This occurs because of changes in the egg white's proteins.

In a raw egg white, individual folded proteins can pass by each other and light can pass through them. As the heat of cooking causes the proteins to unfold and link together, they become less mobile and solidify. The space between them shrinks and light reflects off them, giving the cooked egg its opaque white color. And, if you cook it too long, the egg white becomes leathery!

HYDROLYSIS

During the process of hydrolysis, a molecule splits into two parts when a water molecule is added. For example, when the sugar sucrose undergoes hydrolysis, it breaks into glucose and fructose. On its own, hydrolysis of sugar sucrose in water occurs very slowly. But adding an acid such as lemon juice or vinegar, which acts as a catalyst, can speed up the process of hydrolysis. Heating the solution also speeds the chemical reaction.

RATE OF REACTION

Now that we understand how cooking is a series of chemical reactions in food, it is important to understand everything that can affect the timing of those reactions.

Rate of reaction is the speed at which a chemical reaction occurs. In cooking, factors such as temperature, concentration, catalysts, surface area, and the nature of the substance all affect how quickly or slowly a chemical reaction occurs. In order to control a reaction in cooking, a chef can manipulate these variables.

Nearly all reaction rates increase at higher temperatures, when molecules in food move faster, collide more, and react more. This means if a chef wants to cook an egg faster, they can increase the heat. The more heat added, the faster the egg cooks.

In a similar way, increasing the concentration of certain ingredients, or reactants, can speed up the rate of a reaction. Concentration is a measure of how much of a substance is in a solution. A higher concentration means that more of a substance is in the solution.

This chef is using a very high heat!

The more molecules that are present, the more likely they will collide, and the faster the reaction will go.

Adding a catalyst to a recipe can either speed or slow the rate of reaction. For example, bakers sometimes add vitamin C as a catalyst to speed the chemical reactions that form the protein gluten in baked goods.

Increasing the surface area of a solid substance can also speed the rate of reaction.

With an increased surface area, a greater number of molecules are exposed and more likely to collide with other reactants, which speeds the reaction. Chefs learn how to use these different tools to make their food more quickly and efficiently and taste even more delicious.

ACID AND BASE REACTIONS

Red cabbage juice changes color when lime juice or baking soda is added to it. Baking powder causes a cake to rise in the oven. Lemon and lime juice cook fish into a delicious ceviche. Each of these is an example of an acid/base reaction in the kitchen. Acid/base reactions have many similarities, even though their effects—a color change, rising cake, or cooked fish—can look very different.

Many foods are either acidic or basic, also called alkaline. A substance's pH, which can run from 0 to 14, determines whether it is acidic or basic. Foods below 7 on the pH scale are acidic, foods with a pH of 7 are neutral, and those with a pH above 7 are basic.

In many cases, the sour taste in a food is caused by acids. Fruits such as oranges and lemons are acidic. Carbonated beverages, tea, yogurt, and buttermilk are also acidic.

Acids can be used to denature foods that have a lot of proteins. For example, a fish appetizer called ceviche is cooked in lime juice. The juice's acids break down the proteins in the fish and cause them to denature, or unfold. This gives the ceviche an appealing texture and an opaque color that looks like fish cooked with heat.

When tough meats are soaked in marinades made with vinegar, lemon juice, or other acids, these acids denature the meat proteins.

When water molecules collect in between the denatured proteins, the meat **becomes more tender and flavorful.**

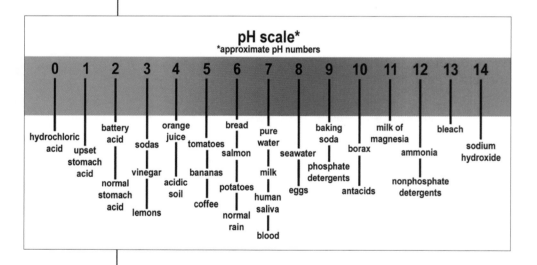

The opposite of an acidic food is one that is basic. Baking soda is a food ingredient that is basic. Bases such as baking soda are used in baking.

When baking soda combines with an acid, it creates a reaction that produces gas bubbles that cause the batter to rise. That's how we get puffy cupcakes!

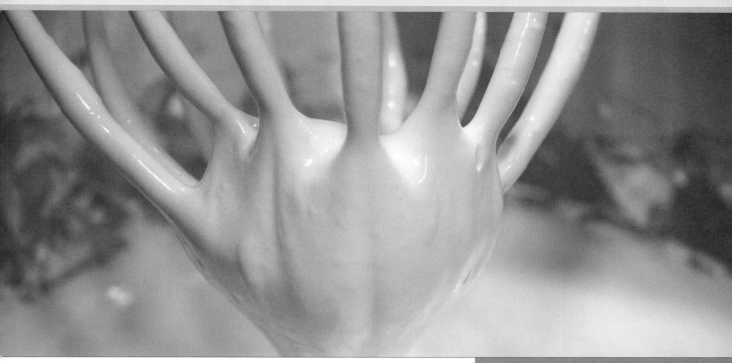

Beaten egg whites

PUT IT ALL TOGETHER—
IN A CAKE!

You might not think of baking a cake as a science experiment, but chemistry is at the core of how flour, sugar, eggs, water, and butter combine into a moist, airy cake. Baking is a series of complex chemical reactions.

One of the first steps in many baked goods recipes is to cream together butter and sugar. The process of creaming creates a simple mixture of butter and sugar. It also adds air. The butter forms a layer around the air pockets to make the mixture light and fluffy. Next, the baker adds egg to the butter-sugar mixture. When beaten, egg whites give dough a light, fluffy texture. Egg whites contain lecithin, which is a protein that also coats the air bubbles created during beating. This prevents the batter from collapsing when baking in the oven. Lecithin also acts as a binder to hold the cake together.

BAKING

Almost all recipes for baked goods include flour, eggs, a fat such as butter or oil, sugar, and a leavening agent such as baking soda or powder. Using these ingredients, the baker follows a specific sequence of steps to trigger chemical change and produce a delicious baked treat.

Watch this video from NBC News to learn about the chemistry of bread-making!

What chemical reactions are taking place in the bread?

the chemistry of bread

FOOD FACT

Why does raw batter taste different from the baked cake? Chemical reactions from heat create flavor compounds and aromas that mixing cannot produce!

Another main ingredient in breads, cookies, cakes, and other baked goods is flour, a powdered form of grains, nuts, or beans. Wheat flour is one of the most commonly used flours in baking. It is mostly starch and two proteins: glutenin and gliadin. When mixed with water, these two proteins bond together and form a new protein, called gluten.

Gluten gives baked goods structure because the protein's strands **form an elastic network around the air bubbles in the dough.**

Gluten helps the baked good hold its shape. As the baker mixes flour and water, gluten molecules form and become elongated. They organize into a type of webbing that is both stretchy and able to hold a shape. Chains of gluten grow longer and stronger as more molecules stick together.

Bakers also add a leavening agent, such as baking powder, baking soda, or yeast, to their dough. Leavening agents give baked goods a light, airy texture. When heated, the leavening agents undergo chemical reactions that release carbon dioxide gas into the dough or batter.

One common agent, baking soda, undergoes a chemical reaction with acids in the dough. The reaction produces carbon dioxide gas as a product. This gas puffs up the dough. Baking powder releases tiny bubbles of carbon dioxide gas twice—once when it mixes with water and again when it is heated to a certain temperature during baking. The carbon dioxide gas causes the dough to rise and gives it a light, delicate texture.

As the dough or batter is heated further, the water in the batter from the butter and eggs begins to change into a vapor. As the vapor expands, it expands the existing air bubbles in the batter. The gluten network prevents the gas from escaping and holds the baked good together.

As the heat rises, the proteins in the egg coagulate, the flour's starch absorbs any remaining moisture, and the gluten begins to lose its elasticity. At this point, the batter is "set" and takes on its final shape.

KEY QUESTIONS

- **What is the difference between caramelization and Maillard reactions?**
- **Why is it important to know which ingredients are acids and which are bases when baking?**
- **How do the three different kinds of heat transfer work together during cooking?**

BAKING'S BROWNING REACTIONS

When baking at high temperatures, browning reactions give baked goods color and flavor. In baking, the Maillard reaction breaks down amino acids in proteins and sugars in the batter and rearranges the molecules into new substances. The reaction creates organic compounds that darken the surface of baked dough.

Caramelization also occurs during the baking process. This chemical reaction causes sugar molecules in the batter to break down and release water. Heat causes the water to turn into steam and produces new flavor compounds. Both the Maillard reaction and caramelization work together to create an appealing golden-brown color and a variety of delicious flavors in baked goods.

Finally, after all of the physical and chemical reactions are complete, the baked good is ready to enjoy!

TEXT TO WORLD

Have you ever had unleavened bread? How is it different from yeast bread?

LEMON CURD AND PROTEIN DENATURATION

Protein denaturation occurs when protein molecules unwind from their naturally folded shape. Denaturation is usually caused by heat, but can also be caused by freezing or adding acid, salt, or baking soda. When protein molecules are heated, they unfold and extend into a long protein chain. Exposed parts of the molecule can now bond with other protein molecules. These bonds cause clumping and thickening as the molecules draw closer together. In this activity, we will explore how proteins denature as we make lemon curd.

Lemon curd is a creamy mixture made from lemon juice, sugar, butter, and eggs. When the ingredients are cooked, the mixture thickens. When it cools, the thickened lemon curd can be used as a spread, topping, or filling for many desserts.

CAUTION: Ask an adult to help you with the zester, knife, and stove.

Ingredients ▼

- 3 lemons
- 1 cup sugar
- ½ cup butter
- 3 eggs

- **Wash the lemons and zest one using a grater or zester.** Put the lemon zest in the saucepan.

- **Using a cutting board, cut each of the lemons in half and squeeze the juice out of them into a small bowl.** Make sure no seeds are included.

- **Add the lemon juice, butter, and sugar to a saucepan and put the pan on the stove on very low heat.** Stir the mixture until the sugar is mostly dissolved and the butter melts.

- **Crack the three eggs into a small bowl and mix.** Then, add the eggs to the lemon mixture and whisk.

- **Cook the mixture over medium-low heat for about 10 to 20 minutes, stirring continuously.** Watch your mixture closely as curds easily overcook. You want the mixture to thicken to the consistency of a thin pudding. What is happening in the food to cause it to thicken?

- **Once the curd reaches the right consistency, remove it from heat.** You can strain it through a strainer to remove the lemon zest if you want, but you don't need to. Let it cool for about five minutes and then pour it into small bowls or serving containers. You can eat the lemon curd by itself, spread it on a scone or toast, or add it as a filling to another dessert.

- **As you enjoy the dessert, think about the following questions.**

  - What are the two components in this recipe that cause proteins in the egg to denature?

  - What would happen if you cook the mixture for too long or at too high a temperature?

  - What role does sugar play in this recipe? How does it affect the egg proteins?

To investigate more, try making this recipe with a different type of citrus fruit. Does changing the fruit affect the final product? What differences, if any, do you observe? Why?

CARAMELIZATION OF SUGAR

One of the most common chemical changes in cooking is the caramelization of sugar. Observe the changes that occur firsthand.

CAUTION: Ask an adult to help you with this activity. The extremely hot sugar mixture can cause burns.

- **Mix the sugar and water in a small saucepan and stir until the sugar dissolves in the water.** How does the solution look, smell, and taste? Record your observations in your science journal.

- **Place the saucepan over high heat on a stove and heat the solution.** Use a candy thermometer to track the solution's temperature.

- **Every time the solution increases 50 degrees Fahrenheit, take a spoonful out and put it on a heat-resistant plate.** Label the plates with the temperatures and set them aside to cool. Take the last spoonful of the mixture when there has been no significant increase in temperature for at least three minutes. Turn off the heat and remove the saucepan from the stove.

- **After the material on the plates has cooled, examine each one.** What does it look like? How does it smell? How does it taste? Describe the flavor of each. What happens to the sweetness? How do you explain your observations?

> To investigate more, try this activity using brown sugar. What do you observe? Are there any differences between white and brown sugar? You may also want to try this activity using a recipe for caramel sauce that includes butter and milk. What do you observe?

Ingredients ▼

- 1⅓ cups white sugar
- ⅔ cup water

VOCAB LAB

Write down what you think each word means. What root words can you find to help you? What does the context of the word tell you?

caramelization, conduction, convection, leavening agent, Maillard reaction, radiant heat, and **rate of reaction.**

Compare your definitions with those of your friends or classmates. Did you all come up with the same meanings? Turn to the text and glossary if you need help.

MAKE CARAMELIZED CARROTS

Caramelization can occur in any food that contains carbohydrates. Carbohydrates come in many forms, from the natural sugars in fruits and vegetables to processed sugars such as table sugar. Carrots are naturally high in sugar, making them a good choice for caramelizing.

Ingredients ▼

- carrots
- olive oil
- salt
- pepper

- **Peel carrots and cut them into smaller pieces.** Put aside one raw carrot. Coat the remaining carrots in olive oil and spread in a single layer on a baking sheet. Add salt and pepper to taste.

- **Roast carrots at 400 degrees Fahrenheit (204 degrees Celsius).** Every 10 minutes, remove a carrot and put it aside. Label the carrot with the time it cooked. Roast the carrots for a total of 25 to 40 minutes—stirring them halfway through the roasting time—until they begin to caramelize on the edges and are easily pierced with a fork.

- **When done, remove the baking sheet from the oven and serve the carrots immediately.** Cover, refrigerate, and eat any leftover carrots within three to four days.

- **Compare the raw carrot, the carrots removed during cooking, and the final caramelized carrots.** What differences do you observe in appearance, color, texture, aroma, taste, and flavor? What causes these differences?

> To investigate more, try caramelizing other vegetables, such as potatoes, broccoli, mushrooms, and onions. What differences do you find between the cooked vegetables? Which have more natural sugar?

HOW MUCH GLUTEN IS IN THAT FLOUR?

Gluten is very important in baking and gives baked goods their structure. Gluten forms when proteins in flour mix with water and bond together. Different flours have different amounts of proteins. A high-protein flour makes a dough with strong gluten, which is good for baking hearty breads. A low-protein flour is a better choice for delicate pastry dough.

In this activity, you'll test different types of flour to see how much gluten forms and discover why different flours are better for different recipes.

- **Measure 1 cup of each flour in three separate bowls and label each.**

- **Add ½ cup of water to each bowl.** Slowly knead each mixture until it forms a soft, rubbery ball of dough.

Ideas for Supplies ▼

- 3 types of flour, such as white, wheat, and semolina
- water
- cheesecloth

- **Let the dough rest for at least 10 minutes.** What is happening during this rest period? Record your observations in your science journal.

- **After the rest period, fill one of the bowls with water to cover the dough ball.** Squeeze the dough gently to remove the starch from it. For more delicate flours, you may want to hold the dough in cheesecloth during this step. What happens to the water? Why?

- **Pour out the cloudy water and replace with fresh water.** Continue gentle kneading until the water no longer becomes cloudy. What has happened to the dough ball? Can you stretch it?

- **Repeat this process for each type of flour.** How does the texture of each one change as you rinse away the starch? How long does it take for each type of flour? Are the dough balls all the same size or are they different sizes? Record your observations.

- **Next, try baking the gluten balls in the oven for about 15 to 20 minutes at 450 degrees Fahrenheit (232 degrees Celsius).** What happens to each? Record your observations.

- **What can you conclude from this experiment?** Which type of dough has the most gluten? Which has the least? How can you use this information to decide which flour to use when baking?

> To investigate more, try this activity using gluten-free flour. What happens? Use the internet to research what ingredients replace gluten in gluten-free baking.

Inquire & Investigate

GLUTEN INTOLERANCE

For some people, eating foods with gluten can be an unpleasant experience. Gluten causes an immune response in the body for people with celiac disease that damages the small intestine lining. Celiac disease symptoms include diarrhea, constipation, abdominal pain, weight loss, bloating, and itchy skin. People who do not have intestinal damage but experience similar symptoms may have gluten sensitivity. People with either condition should avoid eating foods with gluten.

COOKIES AND RATES OF REACTION

Everyone likes their cookies a little different. Some prefer chewy cookies, while others prefer crispy cookies. How can you use science to make the perfect cookie? In this activity, you'll test how time and temperature affect the rates of reaction when baking cookies. You'll need a light-colored cookie dough, either homemade or store-bought.

CAUTION: Ask an adult to help you with the oven.

- **Choose the time and temperature ranges that you want to test.** For example, you could choose to test three temperatures and four baking times as shown in this chart.

TEMPERATURE (IN FAHRENHEIT)	TIME (IN MINUTES)				
300 degrees	6	9	12	15	18
350 degrees	6	9	12	15	18
400 degrees	6	9	12	15	18

- **Preheat the oven to the lowest temperature to be tested.** Scoop five spoonfuls of dough onto a baking sheet lined with parchment paper. Put the baking sheet in the oven and set the timer for the shortest time on the table (6 minutes). When time is reached, remove one cookie and set it aside to cool. Make sure to label the cooled cookies so you know the time/temperature for each. What reactions are taking place in the cookies as they bake?

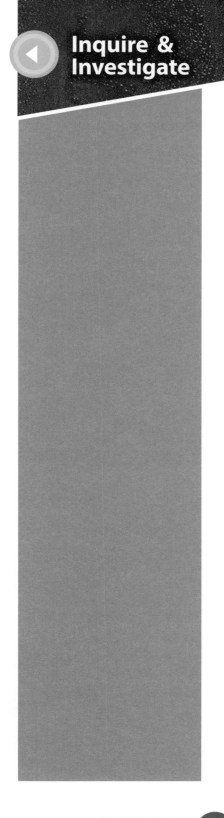

- **Bake another 3 minutes until the next time variable (9 minutes) is reached.** Remove another cookie. Repeat this process until all cookies for this temperature are baked.

- **Increase the oven's temperature for the next temperature variable.** Using a cooled baking sheet, repeat the baking process for five time variables. Repeat for the third temperature variable, again with a cool baking sheet.

- **Compare the cookies baked at the same temperature, but with different times.** What observations can you make?

- **Compare the cookies baked at the same time, but with different temperatures.** What do you observe?

- **Compare the lowest-temperature, longest-time cookie to the highest-temperature, shortest-time cookie.** What do you notice about the differences in the color in these cookies? What differences in color exist between the edges and centers? What causes this?

- **What conclusion can you make about the variables of time and temperature when baking cookies?** What effect does each have on rates of reaction in the cookies? In your opinion, what combination creates the perfect cookie? Record all of your observations and conclusions in your science journal.

> To investigate more, think about what would happen if you used a different type of cookie dough. Would decreasing the amount of sugar or adding an acid such as lemon or orange juice affect the rates of reaction in the cookie?

USE SALT AND ICE TO MAKE ICE CREAM

Did you know that you can use salt to make ice cream? When table salt (NaCl) dissolves in water (H_2O), it triggers an endothermic reaction, a chemical reaction that takes in heat and decreases the temperature of the surrounding area. The salt's sodium (Na) and chloride (Cl) atoms break apart. Breaking these bonds requires energy and cools down the surrounding water. In this activity, we'll take our knowledge of this chemical reaction and use it to make ice cream.

Ideas for Supplies ▼

- 1 small resealable plastic bag, quart-size
- 1 large resealable plastic bag, gallon size
- 12 ice cubes
- 1 cup salt
- ½ cup heavy cream
- ½ cup milk
- 2 tablespoons sugar
- ½ teaspoon vanilla extract

- **Put the heavy cream, milk, sugar, and vanilla extract into the small plastic bag and seal it.** Leave a small pocket of air inside the bag.

- **Next, add the ice and salt to the larger bag.** Then, place the smaller, sealed bag into the larger bag and seal the larger bag.

- **Shake it up!** Massage and shake the bag. If your hands get too cold, put on a pair of gloves or use a towel to hold the bag.

- **After a few minutes, open the large bag and use a thermometer to measure and record the temperature of the salty ice water.** Continue shaking and massaging the bag for about 10 minutes, until the mixture in the smaller bag looks like soft-serve ice cream. Use the thermometer to measure and record the temperature of the salty water.

- **Remove the smaller bag, rinse it, and open it.** Take a spoonful of the ice cream. What does it taste like? What is its texture? What do you think would have happened if you had used another compound instead of salt?

> **To investigate more,** test what effect different ratios of salt and water have on the ability to make ice cream. Create a chart that shows each ratio, the temperature measurements during the activity, and the final results.

Chapter 3

Nutrition: What Makes Food Healthy?

Why are some foods considered healthier than others?

The body gets certain nutrients from food to function healthily. Some foods have more of what our bodies need, while other foods have very little nutritional value. It's important to find a balance so your body can perform as well as possible!

Just as a cell phone needs to be recharged, so does the human body. We eat food and drink water every day to give our bodies the energy and nutrients we need to grow and function. Nutrients in food include proteins, carbohydrates, fats, vitamins, minerals, fiber, and water.

If you do not eat the right balance of nutrients, your body will not function properly. You may also be at a higher risk of developing certain health conditions.

Nutrition is the study of the nutrients in food and drink and how they affect the human body. Nutritionists investigate how the body breaks down and uses nutrients in food to function and grow. Nutritionists also look at the relationships among food, nutrients, health, and disease. They study how food choices can reduce or increase the risk of disease and what happens in the body if we have too much or too little of a nutrient.

To better understand nutrition, let's look deeply into the chemical makeup of our foods and discover how our bodies process and use these foods.

PROTEIN: THE BODY'S BUILDING BLOCKS

The human body needs three major macronutrients—carbohydrates, proteins, and fats—in large amounts to function properly. These macronutrients provide the basic building blocks and fuel for all of the body's processes.

Did you eat enough protein today? The trillion cells in the human body include thousands of proteins. Together, these proteins act like tiny machines inside the cell to allow the cell to do its job. Proteins are involved in nearly every biological process. Many proteins build, strengthen, repair, and replace body structures and tissues. Some proteins, such as collagen and keratin, are structural. Collagen provides support for the body's connective tissues, including cartilage. Keratin strengthens the body's protective coverings, such as hair and fingernails.

Other proteins create the body's chemical messengers, called hormones.

Insulin is a hormone that allows the sugar glucose in the blood to enter the body's cells, which gives them the energy they need to function properly. Other proteins function as carriers—hemoglobin is a red blood cell that carries oxygen in the blood to all of the body's cells.

Keratin protein

VITAMINS AND MINERALS

Vitamins and minerals are micronutrients the body needs in small amounts to support overall health. They have an important role in cell metabolism and neurological functions. Vitamins and minerals help the body produce energy, heal wounds, and form bones. Vitamins and minerals also play roles in the immune system and eye and skin health. For example, vitamin A helps maintain healthy vision, while vitamin C helps heal wounds and assists the body in fighting germs.

Proteins have several vital roles in the body. They help repair and build tissues, allow metabolic reactions to occur, provide structure in the body, and much more.

Check out this video to learn more about why proteins are so important in your body!

how the body
uses proteins

Some proteins are enzymes. Enzymes function as catalysts in the body and speed up chemical reactions. Enzymes are essential for cellular respiration, which is the process of the body using oxygen to get energy from the food we eat.

What foods are good sources of protein? Protein is found in beef, pork, chicken, other meats, fish and seafood, eggs, soybeans, and certain legumes. While we talk about eating foods with protein, what the body really needs is amino acids. There are nine essential amino acids that the human body does not make itself, so they must come from food.

These amino acids are: histidine, isoleucine, leucine, lysine, methionine, phenylalanine, threonine, tryptophan, and valine. Without these amino acids, the body cannot make the proteins it needs to function properly.

Not all protein foods are created equal! Foods can contain complete **proteins, incomplete proteins, or complementary proteins.**

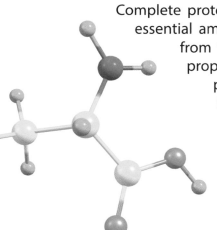

Complete proteins contain all nine essential amino acids we need from food in adequate proportions. Complete proteins are generally found in animal-based foods such as meats, dairy, and eggs. Some complete proteins are found in plant-based sources, including quinoa and soy.

A model of a molecule of methionine, an essential amino acid

Incomplete proteins have at least one essential amino acid, but not all of them. Plant foods such as beans, peas, and grains generally supply incomplete protein. Sometimes, two or more foods with incomplete proteins can be combined to supply the body with complete protein. Together, they are called complementary proteins. Examples of complementary proteins include peanut butter and whole grain bread or whole grain rice and red beans.

EAT YOUR PROTEINS!

How much protein does the average adult need to eat daily? The U.S. Food and Drug Administration (FDA) recommends that teenagers eat 46 to 52 grams of protein daily as part of a 2,400-calorie diet. That daily amount may vary by person depending on their age, calorie needs, gender, activity level, and other factors. A lack of protein in the diet can lead to health problems such as loss of muscle mass, increased risk of bone fractures, and skin, hair, and nail problems.

Quinoa is a great substitute for rice or pasta!

You do not need to eat all the essential amino acids at every meal. Your body can combine amino acids from meals throughout the day to form complete proteins.

FOOD FACT

Refined grains such as white flour, white bread, and white rice have been processed to give them a fine texture and longer shelf life. However, the processing also removes dietary fiber and many vitamins and minerals from these foods.

CARBOHYDRATES PROVIDE ENERGY

Do you know someone who is "watching their carbs?" Recent diet trends tout limiting or even eliminating carbohydrates from the diet in order to lose weight and feel healthy. However, the human body needs carbohydrates to function properly and grow. Carbohydrates provide energy, giving the body the fuel it needs to run, jump, and move. The body also needs energy to grow. Even when you are resting, your body uses energy to maintain body temperature, keep your heart beating, and digest food.

Simple carbohydrates, such as the sugars found in milk, fruits, syrups, and white bread, can be broken down quickly and absorbed by the body. The digestive process converts the sugars in food into glucose. The stomach and small intestines absorb glucose molecules and release them into the bloodstream. The blood carries glucose to cells throughout the body to be used for energy.

Starch is another type of carbohydrate found in many foods. Because starch molecules are larger and more complex than sugar molecules, it takes the body longer to break down and absorb these complex carbohydrates. Eating unprocessed starches—such as peas, corn, potatoes, beans, oats, barley, brown rice, wheat, and other whole grains—can make you feel full for longer.

FOOD FACT

The liver stores excess glucose that can be released when blood glucose levels fall low. If the glucose supply exceeds what the liver can hold, the glucose is turned into body fat for long-term storage. When carbohydrates are scarce, the body breaks down some of its fat stores for energy.

Which nutrient gives you the energy needed to run a marathon—proteins, fats, or carbohydrates?

Watch this video to find out!

carbs vs. protein for endurance

Fiber is another type of complex carbohydrate. Fiber comes from cell walls in plants and can be found in fruits, vegetables, whole grains, nuts, dried beans, peas, and lentils. Soluble fiber dissolves in water and can be broken down by the body and used for energy. Soluble fiber also helps reduce the risk of heart disease and diabetes and promotes gut health. Other types of fiber, called insoluble fibers, cannot be absorbed into the bloodstream and pass through the body. Although insoluble fibers do not provide nutrients, they do have an important function.

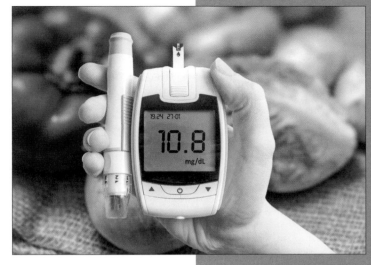

Diabetics need to check their blood sugar and regulate their insulin levels.

Fiber helps waste material move through the intestines. Eating enough fiber can prevent constipation.

Unlike proteins, there are no essential carbohydrates that humans need to eat. However, the human body must have glucose circulating in the bloodstream to provide energy for the body's functions. The body regulates the level of glucose in the blood using hormones called insulin and glucagon.

Although carbohydrates are an important energy source for the body, eating too many carbohydrates can cause a variety of health problems. Foods that are high in sugars, such as cakes, cookies, candies, and white bread, provide a quick source of energy. However, eating too much of them can lead to weight gain and its related health problems.

Sometimes, the body is unable to properly regulate glucose in the bloodstream. Diabetes is a disease that occurs when you cannot maintain normal glucose levels in the blood. Too much glucose can lead to blindness, nerve damage, or blood vessel damage. Too little glucose can cause fainting, seizures, brain damage, and even death.

FATS: NECESSARY TO THRIVE

Fats, also called lipids, are one of the macronutrients the human body needs to function properly. Without fats, you could not live. Fats supply us with energy.

Fats provide twice the energy per gram as carbohydrates and supply more than half of the body's energy needs.

Fat from foods breaks down into fatty acids during digestion and travels through the blood to cells. Fats help other nutrients do their jobs. They provide structure to cells, help lubricate joints, and help organs produce hormones. They assist the body in absorbing certain vitamins, such as vitamin A, a nutrient needed for healthy eyes and lungs. Fats also play a role in reducing inflammation in the body and maintaining brain health. Unsaturated fats, including omega-3 fats, are particularly healthy. These are usually liquid at room temperatures, and they are often derived from plants and oily fish.

When the body has excess fatty acids or glucose, it stores them as body fat. Body fat stores energy for times when you do not have enough food for energy. It can be burned to keep the body warm and forms padding to protect organs. But eating too many calories for a long time can cause you to add excess body fat. The additional body fat causes stress on the heart, muscles, and other organs. Too much fat can lead to health problems, including heart disease, obesity, and liver disease.

Fats in food come in several forms. Vegetable fats are typically liquid and are found in oils such as olive oil, peanut oil, and corn oil. Animal fats are usually solid and include butter, lard, cream, and the fat found on certain meats.

Our bodies need fat to function properly. But did you know that not all fats are created equal? Some fats are considered healthy, while other fats are unhealthy. Eating too many unhealthy fats can lead to a variety of health problems, from obesity to heart disease.

Take a look at this video to learn more about the types of fats in your food and how the different types of fat impact your health.

what is fat
George Zaidan

WATER: A DELICATE BALANCE

Water is a major part of most foods we eat, especially fruits and vegetables. The body absorbs the water through the digestive tract. How much water you need depends on your size, age, activity level, health status, and environmental conditions. For example, if you exercise in the heat, you need to drink more water to replace water lost through sweat than if you are reading a book in an air-conditioned room.

Healthy kids should drink at least 2 quarts of water each day.

Doctors use images like this to show us the types of different foods and the quantities we should be eating for optimal health.

When you consume too little water, you can become dehydrated. Signs of dehydration include thirst and reduced and dark-colored urine. If you become very dehydrated, you may also breathe faster and have a higher pulse rate, as well as experience muscle spasms and nausea.

On the other hand, if you consume too much water, your body's electrolytes can become diluted. Electrolytes are forms of minerals the body needs to stay in balance and maintain blood pressure.

FOOD FACT

• • • • • • • • • • • •

The human body is up to 60 percent water.

HOW WE GET NUTRIENTS FROM FOOD

How does the body turn a plate of spaghetti and meatballs into something its cells can use? It all happens in the body's digestive system. The digestive system includes your mouth, teeth, esophagus, stomach, small and large intestines, and rectum. From the moment you take a bite of food, the body works on a series of chemical reactions to break down the food into the necessary nutrients and components.

To see how the process of digestion happens in the body, let's follow that bite of spaghetti. You use your teeth to chew the spaghetti and break it down into smaller parts. Chewing food makes it easier to swallow. It also increases the surface area of the food, which helps the digestive process later.

Don't forget to drink plenty of water when playing sports!

While you chew, the spaghetti mixes with saliva in your mouth. Salivary glands in your cheeks and under the jaw and tongue release saliva. Saliva contains enzymes that break down the cell walls of food. These enzymes start changing the complex carbohydrates in the spaghetti into simpler carbohydrates and sugars.

Once you've chewed the spaghetti enough, you swallow it. It passes from the mouth down the throat through a tube called the esophagus. Gravity propels food down the esophagus, while muscular contractions in the esophagus also push the food to your stomach. A muscle outside the stomach forces the food inside it.

When the spaghetti arrives in the stomach, the real work begins to break it down into usable molecules. The stomach contains strong acids and enzymes to break down food. These acids are so strong that a layer of mucus lines the stomach to protect it from its own digestive acids.

Layers of muscle in the stomach wall pull in three directions and churn the food like clothes in a washing machine.

The spaghetti stays in your stomach for a few hours, until it has a creamy, liquid consistency. When finished in the stomach, this liquid is gradually squirted into the small intestine.

The small intestine is a long, thin tube that winds and snakes around your lower abdomen. In the small intestine, the spaghetti mixes with bile and other enzymes produced by the liver and pancreas that further break down the food. Here, the spaghetti is finally broken down into simple molecules such as glucose, amino acids, simple fatty acids, vitamins, and minerals.

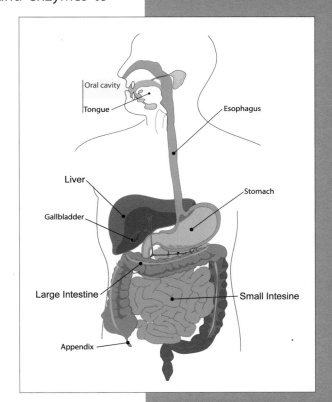

Oral cavity
Tongue
Esophagus
Liver
Stomach
Gallbladder
Large Intestine
Small Intesine
Appendix

The human digestive system

The wall of the small intestine absorbs these molecules and moves them into the blood. Once in the blood, the nutrients travel through the bloodstream to the liver for processing.

Meanwhile, muscular contractions in the intestine wall propel the food through the small intestine. The entire process takes about three to six hours. After traveling through the small intestine, what's left of the spaghetti continues to the large intestine and exits the body through the rectum.

What happens to those nutrients that the blood moved to the liver? The liver is like a manufacturing plant that filters, processes, manufactures, and stores nutrients.

It breaks down fat and makes glucose from carbohydrates. The liver makes sure the right nutrients are sent to the correct parts of the body. It also filters and flushes out toxic substances, such as pollutants, bacterial toxins, and other chemicals.

In addition, the liver stockpiles nutrients, primarily vitamins, minerals, and glycogen. Glycogen is a form of stored glucose. When the body needs energy, the liver converts stored glycogen into glucose and sends it into the blood. Stored nutrients allow your body to survive without food for days—even weeks! The nutrients also serve as a backup in case your diet does not contain a necessary nutrient.

TURNING FOOD INTO ENERGY

Have you ever felt tired before lunch? That's because your body needs energy to power it! You need energy to play basketball, concentrate during chemistry class, and do all your daily activities.

The digestive system is one of the human body's most complicated systems. Its numerous parts work together to digest food and break it into the nutrients and energy the body needs. Want to learn more about this incredible system?

Watch this video about the digestive system's work!

Emma Bryce
digestive system

Even basic body functions require energy. That energy comes from the nutrients in the food you eat. Your body digests food and breaks it down into usable molecules of carbohydrates, proteins, and fats.

Carbohydrate molecules break down into a simple sugar molecule called glucose. Glucose is a cell's main source of energy. To use glucose for energy, the body's cells must change it into a usable form. They do this in a process called cellular respiration.

For cellular respiration to occur, a cell must have two ingredients: glucose and oxygen. You breathe in oxygen and get glucose from food. Cellular respiration takes the glucose and oxygen molecules and combines them to create carbon dioxide, water, and energy in the form of ATP (adenosine triphosphate).

ATP is a high-energy molecule found in every cell. It stores and supplies the cell with energy. When a cell needs energy to perform its specific task, it turns to ATP molecules in its cytoplasm, the jellylike fluid in the cell.

MAKING ATP

Cellular respiration involves three main stages: glycolysis, the Krebs cycle, and the electron transport chain. In glycolysis, the cell converts glucose into a chemical called pyruvate and two molecules of ATP. In the Krebs cycle, the cell converts the pyruvate into some energy-storing molecules and two more molecules of ATP. Finally, in the electron transport chain, the cell takes the energy-storing molecules created earlier and combines them with oxygen to create about 34 ATP molecules. In total, the process of cellular respiration creates about 38 molecules of ATP from a single glucose molecule.

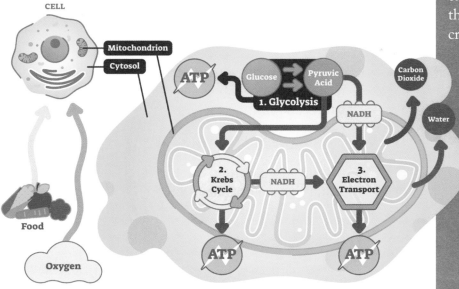

CELL

Mitochondrion

Cytosol

ATP

Glucose

Pyruvic Acid

1. Glycolysis

NADH

Carbon Dioxide

Water

2. Krebs Cycle

NADH

3. Electron Transport

ATP

ATP

Food

Oxygen

TEXT TO WORLD

How healthy is your own diet right now? Are you getting the nutrients you need?

The three phosphate atoms (P) in the ATP molecule are linked together by phosphate bonds. The molecule's energy is locked into these bonds. When the cell needs energy, enzymes within the cell signal the phosphate bonds to break.

KEY QUESTIONS

- Why is it important to stay hydrated, especially when exercising?
- Why did bodies develop the ability to store fat for later use?

When the bonds break, the three phosphate atoms separate from the **ATP molecule and release energy.**

The cell uses this energy to perform chemical or mechanical reactions, such as building proteins. Therefore, ATP gives each cell in the body the energy needed to perform its specific tasks that support life.

Because food provides nutrients that are essential to your body's functioning, healthy food choices can help your body function efficiently. Doctors recommend that you fill your diet with foods such as whole fruits and vegetables, whole grains, low-fat and fat-free dairy, and lean meats. They also recommend limiting the amount of added sugars, salts, and processed foods in your diet.

Eating the right combination of foods can help you maintain a healthy weight, have more energy, and even prevent disease.

WHAT MAKES FOOD HEALTHY?

What exactly is healthy food? Most people agree that fruits and vegetables are healthy. But what about meat, pasta, bread, low-fat cookies, veggie snack crackers, and chicken wings? Different nutritional plans emphasize eating different foods and avoiding others. All claim to be "healthy." But are they? In this activity, you'll select two common eating plans to investigate and determine which (if either) is healthier.

- **To start, select two eating plans to investigate and compare.** Some common eating plans include low fat, low carb, keto, Mediterranean, whole food, high protein, low sodium, high fiber, DASH diet, vegetarian, and vegan.

- **Research the eating plans that you selected.** Think about the following questions.

  - What type of foods are encouraged on the plan? Why?

  - What type of foods are restricted on the plan? Why?

  - Is the plan meant for long- or short-term use?

  - What are the benefits of the plan? What are the drawbacks?

  - Does the plan provide enough of the nutrients that the body needs? Why or why not?

- **Prepare a chart that presents the information you have learned and compares the two eating plans.** Offer a conclusion as to whether or not you believe each eating plan is healthy for the body. Explain your reasoning.

> To investigate more, design your own healthy eating plan. What foods will you encourage people to eat? What foods (if any) will you restrict? How does your plan provide the nutrients that the body needs?

NUTRITION AND DISEASE

Around the world, many people suffer from nutrient-linked diseases and conditions. These diseases can be caused by nutrient deficiencies or excesses in the diet, eating disorders, obesity, and chronic diseases such as cardiovascular disease, cancer, type 2 diabetes, and others. In this activity, you'll research a specific nutritional condition and learn how it affects human health.

- **To start, brainstorm a list of nutrient-linked diseases and conditions.** You can use the internet to help you come up with ideas. Select one disease to research in depth.

- **When researching your topic, consider the following questions.**

  - What are the signs and symptoms of this disease?

  - How is it linked to food and nutrition?

  - What is happening in the body on a molecular/cellular level? How does this cause a person's symptoms?

  - What are the short-term and long-term risks of this disease?

  - Can this disease be prevented? How?

  - If the disease is chronic, can food and nutrition improve a person's symptoms?

  - How does nutrition play a role in treating and/or curing this disease? What is happening on a molecular/cellular level?

- **Prepare a presentation to share what you have learned with your class.**

> **To investigate more,** use what you have learned about this nutrient-linked disease to create an eating plan for a person affected by it. How will your eating plan impact the person's health? How easy or difficult will the eating plan be for the average person to follow? Why do you think someone may or may not follow the eating plan?

Chapter 4
Flavor: Mixing It Up

Why do different foods have different flavors?

The simple answer is chemistry! A combination of taste and smell gives food its flavor.

Have you ever wondered why your favorite foods taste so good? Flavor is a big reason! Flavor is why you can't get enough of your grandma's homemade apple pie. It's also why you might not be a big fan of your dad's roasted Brussels sprouts. So, what exactly is flavor and how can we use science to understand it?

Flavor is how something tastes, right? Actually, flavor is a bit more complicated. Taste is just one part of flavor. Smell also plays an important role in creating a food's flavor. To put it simply, taste plus smell equals flavor.

To a lesser extent, flavor also includes texture and temperature. Sometimes, it even includes pain, for example, when you eat spicy food! The brain combines all of these signals from the body's senses. It creates a combined sensation that becomes flavor. Let's give flavor a closer look.

THE CHEMISTRY OF FLAVOR

As we've seen, all foods are made up of chemicals. As a result, everything you taste or smell is a response to the food's chemicals. For example, the distinctive smell of cloves comes from a chemical called eugenol. Another spice, cinnamon, gets its characteristic smell from a chemical compound called cinnamaldehyde.

The main senses that create flavor—taste and smell—are based on chemistry. Chemical reactions that involve our mouth, throat, and nose create the flavors we perceive in food. The process begins when molecules from food travel through the air into the nose or are chewed in the mouth. In both cases, the molecules dissolve in watery mucus. This allows them to bind to and stimulate receptor cells that signal the brain.

FOOD FACT

Scientists are investigating more taste receptors. In the future, they could identify taste receptors for fats, base substances, metals, starches, calcium, and water.

Humans can distinguish about 100,000 different flavors.

TASTING FOOD'S CHEMICALS

The first step in tasting a food begins in the mouth. When you chew food, enzymes in saliva begin the process of digesting food. These enzymes break down the food and release some of its molecules that can be identified. These molecules attach to special taste receptors called taste buds on the tongue and in the mouth and throat.

YUCK!

Is there a specific food that you had a bad experience eating and now cannot stand?

Perhaps you ate a bowl of bean soup when you were a child and then promptly threw up. Now, the thought of that soup makes your stomach twist. You may have developed a taste aversion, which is a strong dislike for a particular food. Taste aversions are generally caused by a bad experience with food, often in childhood. Sometimes, the taste aversion is related to a foodborne illness. Other times, the negative experience is not directly linked to the food. You may have gotten sick from the flu, but a negative association between being sick and the food forms in your mind. You can't stand to eat it.

> **Just as some people can hear or see better than others, people can have different senses of taste and smell.**

The average human has about 10,000 taste buds. Most taste buds are located on the top and sides of the tongue, while some are spread in the mouth and throat. Taste buds are located inside tiny bumps called papillae.

Look at your tongue in the mirror. Do you see lots of little bumps along the sides and tip of your tongue? Can you see larger, flattened bumps near the back of your tongue? These bumps are the papillae, which hold your taste buds. Each papillae can hold between one and 700 taste buds, depending on its location.

Each taste bud contains groups of about 50 to 150 receptor cells bundled together. As you chew food, saliva carries food molecules to the taste receptor cells, and the molecules bind to the taste receptor cells.

Not all taste receptor cells are the same. Each taste receptor has a particular shape.

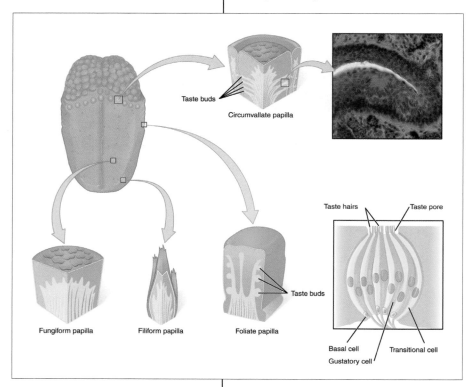

Taste buds
Circumvallate papilla

Fungiform papilla   Filiform papilla   Foliate papilla

Taste hairs   Taste pore

Taste buds

Basal cell   Transitional cell
Gustatory cell

A food molecule can bind only to a taste receptor cell if it fits correctly, like a key fits into a lock. Different food molecules fit into different taste receptor cells.

When the food molecule binds to a receptor, it activates nerve fibers at the bottom of each taste cell to release an electrical signal. The signal travels through the nerves to larger cranial nerves, which carry taste sensations to the brain, where they are interpreted.

How strongly something tastes depends on how much of a chemical compound is in the food we eat. It also depends on how sensitive we are to that compound.

In addition, humans are wired to be more sensitive to certain compounds. Most humans can detect sour, bitter, and irritating compounds in much smaller amounts than salty or sweet compounds. Humans have evolved to recognize sour and bitter tastes as signals that a food may not be safe, has spoiled, or is poisonous.

Being able to detect warning tastes such as bitter and sour in the smallest amounts helps to protect us from dangerous food.

A NOSE FOR FLAVOR

Even though taste and smell are two different senses, they often work together to create our perception of flavor and aroma, especially with food. Food molecules enter your mouth when you eat and also waft into your nose. As taste receptors send sensory information to the brain, the nose also gathers sensory information.

Food molecules enter the nose in one of two ways. First, volatile food molecules floating in the air are drawn into the nose each time you take a breath. Also, when you chew food, volatile molecules are released into the oral cavity and travel through the nasopharynx, or the upper part of the throat, to the nasal cavity.

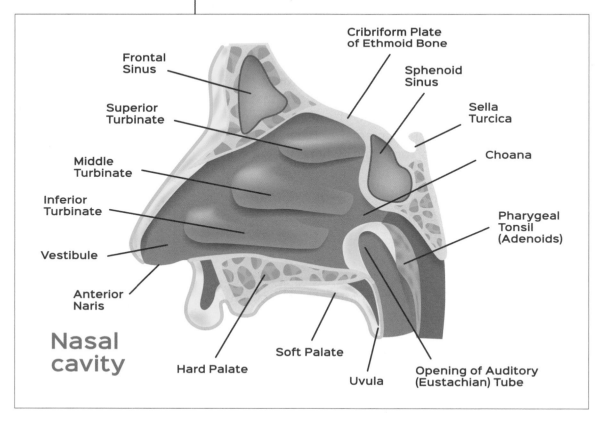

Nasal cavity

Inside the nose, specialized sensory olfactory cells line the top of the nasal cavity. Olfactory cells have receptors that bind to odor molecules. Each receptor has a particular shape, and just as taste molecules fit specific taste receptors, odor molecules must fit into their receptors perfectly so they can bind. When the odor molecule binds to a receptor, it activates the olfactory neuron to fire an electrical signal to the brain. The brain processes this signal and identifies the chemical, which makes you perceive the smell.

The chemical receptors in the nose and mouth can respond to several molecules that have similar structures. Still, you can tell the difference between thousands of smells and tastes even if they trigger the same receptors. That's because most foods are not made of a single molecule. Foods are complex mixtures and activate different combinations of taste and odor receptors at the same time. This gives each food we eat its own unique chemical flavor.

PERCEIVING FLAVOR

To better understand how we perceive flavor, let's follow food into your mouth. It's late afternoon and you are hungry for a snack. You grab a brightly colored orange. You see and smell the orange zest as you peel it and your mouth starts to water.

As you bite into the first piece, the sweet and tart juice squirts in your mouth. Saliva carries molecules from the orange to taste receptor cells in your taste buds. At the same time, escaping molecules from the orange float through the air into your nose and travel from the mouth through the nasopharynx to reach odor receptors in the nasal cavity.

Did you know that the human nose can detect nearly 1 trillion distinct odors? The olfactory system is a complex network of cells and organs that enable you to tell the difference between the smell of a fresh baked pie and a pan of sizzling bacon.

Watch this video to learn more about the details of how this system works together with the brain to create your perception of smell.

how do we
smell video

FOOD FACT

Scientists believe that humans have hundreds of odor receptors and about 50 to 100 different taste receptors.

The orange's molecules bind to specific receptor molecules in the mouth and nose. As soon as binding occurs, the receptor cells send an electrical signal through the nervous system to the brain.

Within the brain, messages travel from place to place, activating different areas of the brain. Some areas produce memories of previous times eating oranges. Some areas stimulate the motor centers in the brain that control salivation, chewing, and swallowing. Other messages activate brain areas that cause you to say, "Yum!" In this way, the perception of the orange flavor is the result of a complicated pattern of sensory neurons and brain neurons being activated.

THE FIVE BASIC TASTES

How does your tongue taste different foods? Do different parts of your tongue taste foods more strongly?

Take a look at this video and try the simple experiment to see how sensitive your tongue is to the five basic tastes!

the science of taste

Humans can recognize five basic tastes: sweet, salty, sour, bitter, and umami (savory). The ability to sense each of the five basic tastes comes from the chemical receptors in our taste buds on the tongue, roof of the mouth, and back of the throat.

Each type of taste is triggered when specific chemical compounds in food **bind to taste receptors and send a signal through the nervous system to the brain.**

The brain combines these signals with signals from olfactory receptors and perceives the overall flavor.

Do you like salty foods? Salt, or sodium chloride (NaCl), is a necessary part of the human diet. Salt molecules can be broken down in water into atoms of sodium (Na) and chloride (Cl). It's the sodium ions (Na+) that give foods a salty taste. They bind to salty taste receptors on the tongue and in the mouth and throat, triggering a signal to the brain.

Sodium ions are used in many body functions, but too much salt is not good. The human brain recognizes that a little salt makes food taste good, but too much salt tastes bad. This ensures that you eat the right amount of salt that the body needs.

Do you have a sweet tooth? Actually, it's a little more accurate to say you've got a "sweet tongue." Sweet tastes signal the presence of sugar molecules. Many fruits and honey contain natural sugars. Because sweet molecules are generally more complex than sodium ions in salty foods, the taste receptor cells that detect sweetness are also more complex.

These receptor cells connect to sugar molecules at two points to measure sweetness. To do this, the sugar molecule must have a certain shape. Tiny differences in how well the molecules fit into the taste receptor cell affect how sweet a food tastes.

FOOD FACT

Some animals cannot taste sugar. Because some animals such as cats do not normally eat carbohydrates in their natural diet, these animals do not have sweet taste receptors.

For example, sucrose, or table sugar, fits well into the taste receptor cell, while the lactose sugars in milk do not fit as well. That's why table sugar tastes sweeter than milk. How we taste sweetness also depends on how easily a molecule binds to the taste receptors and how long it stays bound. Sucrose has a weak connection to the receptor, which is why it takes a few seconds for us to register its sweet taste.

In comparison, fructose, which is a type of sugar often found in fruit, binds very quickly to sweet taste receptors but also detaches quickly. That's why the sweetness in a strawberry registers quickly, but does not linger very long. How the different compounds bind to taste receptors affect how strong a taste sensation is, how quickly we perceive it, and how long it lasts through time.

The mouth-puckering sensation of sour and tart tastes is caused by acids in citrus fruits, such as lemons and grapefruit, as well as other foods, such as yogurt, sourdough bread, and vinegar. When we eat these foods, hydrogen ions from the acids bind to the sour taste receptors on our tongue and mouth and signal the brain. The more concentrated the hydrogen ions, the more sour the food tastes.

FOOD FACT

Umami is a savory or meaty taste produced by certain amino acids in food. Examples of umami foods include seared meats, aged cheeses, green tea, soy sauce, and cooked tomatoes. Savory taste receptors detect amino acids such as glutamate. Glutamate is the most common compound that triggers savory taste.

In some cases, extreme sourness can be a warning sign that a food is contaminated by bacteria. Like bitter tastes, sour tastes evolved to help humans identify potentially dangerous and spoiled foods.

Do you like bitter foods such as broccoli or Brussels sprouts? If you don't, you're not alone.

Many people do not like foods that taste bitter. Bitter tastes come from about 35 different proteins found in plants. The ability to perceive bitter tastes may have evolved as a protection from poison—some bitter compounds are toxic to humans. However, in small amounts, a little bitter flavor can make foods more interesting. And in some cases, bitter foods are healthy.

Antioxidants in dark chocolate and coffee have a bitter taste, yet they help the body's metabolism and protect against cancer. Molecules in these foods bind to taste receptors that send an electrical signal to the brain that produces the perception of bitter taste.

Humans have between 40 to 80 types of bitter taste receptors.

HOW CAN YOU EAT THAT CHEESE?

Why does one person love goat cheese, while another won't touch it? How can one person eat kale every day, while another prefers iceberg lettuce? It boils down to how each person perceives taste. In every person, many factors—from genes to environment—affect how they perceive taste.

Some people are able to taste certain flavors and foods more strongly than others. These supertasters often have more taste cell receptors and taste buds than other people, which causes them to perceive flavors in food more strongly. Many supertasters are particularly sensitive to the bitter flavors in foods, such as broccoli, coffee, and beer. About 25 percent of people are considered supertasters.

Researchers believe that supertasters are born with their increased ability to detect tastes. Most have a particular gene that increases their perception of bitter tastes and makes them more sensitive to bitter compounds in food and drink.

Take a look at a video about supertasters! Are you a supertaster?

SciShow
supertaster

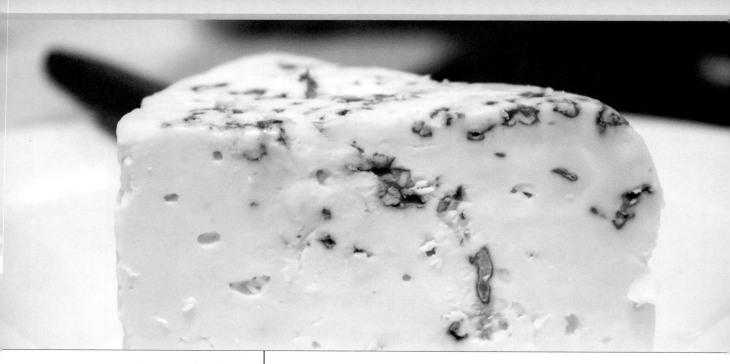

Many people don't like the flavor of blue cheese!

Genetics is one reason two people can experience taste and flavor differently. Your genes affect how taste receptors are configured in your mouth and throat. For example, if you like the flavor of broccoli, you might have fewer bitter taste receptors than your friend who dislikes broccoli's flavor. This difference could result from having different genes that are coded for bitter taste receptors.

Environmental factors can also affect how you taste food.

FOOD FACT

• • • • • • • • • • • • •

A compound's volatility changes with temperature. That's why it's easier to smell warm foods.

The sense of taste can change with the weather. For example, a drier environment changes the amount of saliva in your mouth, which decreases your taste sensitivity. Temperature can also affect taste. Because taste buds are heat-sensitive, taste buds detect flavors in warm foods more strongly than they detect them in cold foods. That's why warm soda tastes so sweet!

What kinds of food did you grow up eating? Your cultural upbringing can affect your sense of taste. Foods that people from one culture enjoy regularly might not taste as delicious to a person from a different culture who is not used to its particular flavors.

For example, Americans typically prefer sweet foods more than Europeans because they are used to eating them. Doughnuts are part of the culture! In Japan, savory foods are more common than they are in other parts of the world.

Sometimes, the taste from one food lingers and impacts the taste of another. Have you ever had a glass of orange juice after brushing your teeth? Ewwww! Why does the sweet juice taste so bitter? The change in your perception of taste occurs because the sodium lauryl sulfate compound in toothpaste lingers in your mouth. It reduces the taste buds' ability to detect the sweetness in the juice. As a result, the orange juice tastes bitter.

One of the symptoms of COVID-19, which caused a widespread pandemic in 2020 and 2021, was the loss of taste and smell.

What kinds of foods have you grown up eating?

COMBINING TASTES AND CHANGING FLAVOR

Combinations of ingredients that have different tastes—such as salty plus sweet or bitter plus sweet—can change food's flavors. For example, adding a small amount of salt to a food can change its flavor by reducing bitterness, which then increases your perception of sweetness. This interaction among different tastes helps to explain why adding an ingredient to a food can boost detection of certain flavors. Sometimes, ingredients can surprise!

Other factors, such as age, stress, and disease, can affect how we experience taste. As humans age, taste perception changes. Anyone who has been around children knows they love to eat sweet foods such as cookies, candies, and cakes. Does that describe you? Children are programmed to prefer sweet tastes because of a biological need for high-calorie foods to support growth and development. As we age, the number of taste buds in our mouths decreases and those remaining begin to shrink. As a result, our ability to detect sweet, salty, sour, and bitter tastes can decline. After age 70, our sense of smell also begins to weaken, which can further affect the experience of tasting foods.

FOOD FACT

Humans may prefer sweet-tasting food because of sugar's ability to provide quick energy.

Stress impacts our experience of taste by increasing the hormone cortisol in the body.

Cortisol decreases the strength of taste buds to detect stimuli. In addition, disease and illness such as the common flu can affect your sense of taste. Have you noticed that food you usually enjoy just doesn't taste right when you're sick?

ADDING FLAVORANTS

In some foods, added flavorants alter or enhance flavors. Flavorants are often added to make foods more appealing or to replace taste that is lost during processing or storage.

Many food producers also add flavorants to make sure that a food product tastes the same no matter where or when it was produced. For example, orange juice manufacturers often add natural and artificial flavorants to the juice after it is packaged at a plant to make sure each bottle tastes the same. This might sound unnecessary, but it's a way to ensure customers always get what they expect.

There are about the same number of chemicals used to make artificial strawberry flavor in a fast food strawberry shake as there are in a fresh strawberry.

Both natural and artificial flavorants contain chemicals. The difference lies in the origin of the flavorant's molecules. Did they come from nature (natural) or were they created in a lab (artificial)? Natural flavorants come from original ingredients found in nature. They are extracted from their source, purified, and then added back to food.

Even though these flavorants are considered "natural," they are still chemicals added to food. For example, a natural flavorant in a strawberry granola bar might be a chemical found in strawberries that has been extracted, enhanced, and added to the granola bar in a laboratory.

Food manufacturers want every one of their products to be the same so people know what they are purchasing.

FOOD FACT

Some natural flavors can be more dangerous that artificial flavors. For example, traces of cyanide, which is toxic in the right amounts, can be found in almond flavor when it comes from a natural source.

WHY IS MY MOUTH BURNING?

Chemical compounds in wing sauce create that burning sensation that feels so good in your mouth! In addition to the primary sensations of taste, taste buds also register sensations related to the chemical properties of food. This is an example of chemesthesis, which occurs when chemical compounds activate sensory receptors that are associated with pain, touch, and perception of heat.

TEXT TO WORLD

Is there a food that you like the smell of but hate the taste?

In comparison, artificial flavorants are human-made. Artificial flavorants are often created to mimic the same chemical compounds found in natural flavorants.

Both natural and artificial flavoring can be made from dozens of ingredients, including preservatives and solvents.

Why use artificial flavorants? Often, artificial flavors are less expensive to make than finding and processing natural flavorants. They can even be safer because they have been tested. For example, the chemical compound vanillin creates the flavor and smell of vanilla. In nature, vanillin can be extracted from the pods of an orchid that grows in Mexico. Extracting this pure, natural chemical is a very long and expensive process. Instead, food scientists developed a way to make a synthetic version of vanillin in a laboratory.

Flavor is a huge part of our experience with food—and so is texture! And what about the way food looks—does that have any influence over how someone approaches it? You bet! Let's take a look at texture and appearance in the next chapter.

KEY QUESTIONS

- Why do we like different flavors at different times in our lives?

- How is the flavor of food related to memory? Does a certain flavor make you think of things from your past?

HOW SMELL AFFECTS FLAVOR

Smell is an integral part of determining a food's flavor. If your sense of smell is impaired, the flavors you detect in food and drink may also be affected. In this activity, you will explore how smell and flavor are linked. You will need five to 10 different food or drink items to test. Try to choose items of similar texture so that texture does not affect the results.

- **Recruit five to 10 volunteers for this activity.** Have each volunteer begin by taking a sip of water to clear any leftover food molecules in their mouth and throat.

- **Have one volunteer put on a nose plug and blindfold.** Ask the volunteer to taste the first item and try to identify it. Record their answer. The volunteer should then take another sip of water to clear their mouth. Next, the volunteer should remove the nose plug and re-taste the food to try to identify it.

- **Repeat this process for each food item and each volunteer.** Make sure to have the volunteers sip water between each taste test.

- **Create a chart or graph to show your results.** When the volunteers plugged their noses, how accurate were they at identifying foods? When they were able to use their sense of smell, did their ability to identify the foods change? Why?

> To investigate more, repeat the experiment with foods of different textures. Does this make a difference in a person's ability to identify the food and flavors? Explain your results.

VOCAB LAB

Write down what you think each word means. What root words can you find to help you? What does the context of the word tell you?

bitter, chemesthesis, extracted, flavorant, fructose, olfactory, papillae, salivation, supertaster, taste receptor, and **umami.**

Compare your definitions with those of your friends or classmates. Did you all come up with the same meanings? Turn to the text and glossary if you need help.

FRESH VS. LEFTOVER PIZZA

A pizza fresh out of the oven is a hot, delicious creation of dough, sauce, cheese, and toppings. When you heat up a leftover slice the next day, the flavor just isn't the same. In this activity, you'll investigate what happens to change the flavor of day-old pizza. This is a good activity to do the day after pizza night!

- **Start with a fresh piece of pizza.** Use your senses to observe the pizza's appearance, aroma, taste, texture, and flavors. Look at it, smell it, taste it. How does it smell? What textures do you detect for the crust, sauce, cheese, and toppings? What tastes can you detect? How would you describe the overall flavor of the fresh pizza? Record your observations in your science journal.

- **The next day, try the day-old pizza.** Use your senses to observe the pizza's appearance, aroma, taste, texture, and flavors. Record your observations.

- **Compare the two slices of pizza.** How are they different? How are they similar? How has the flavor changed? What about the appearance, aroma, and texture?

- **What is happening within the pizza to cause these changes?** To answer this question, think about the following.

  - What are some of the physical and chemical properties that affect the flavor of the pizza and its cheese?

  - How does re-heating the pizza affect these properties? How does this affect flavor?

To investigate more, repeat this experiment with other foods. Which ones taste almost the same when you compare fresh to leftover? Why do you think this occurs? What properties of the foods make their flavors remain the same?

Chapter 5
Texture: What Food Feels Like

How does the look and feel of a food change the experience of eating it?

Texture and appearance have a lot to do with why we choose to eat a certain food or not. We don't usually eat something that looks (and sounds) unappealing!

What comes to mind first when you think of eating an apple? The taste? The way the light shines on the deep red of the skin? The crunch your teeth will make biting into the flesh? All of these elements are part of our experience of eating an apple or any other kind of food.

Eating food is a sensory experience. We study the appearance of a food to decide if we want to try it. We smell its aroma and take a small taste. We evaluate how the food feels in our mouth. Sometimes, we listen to the sound food makes as we eat, such as the crunch of a carrot or the crack of a lobster claw. Taken together, all of these sensory inputs combine to create our experience with food.

HOW DOES IT LOOK?

One of the first sensory inputs that we use to evaluate a food is its appearance. Before we decide to eat a food, we notice its colors, shininess, blemishes, and visual texture.

Sometimes, just one look is enough to make us say "no thank you" to a food. But for some of us, that first glance is enough to start the saliva glands working! Either way, chemistry is part of appearance.

Some of food's colors come from natural pigment in the food. In fresh meat, the red-purplish color comes from myoglobin, which is a red protein found in the muscles of most mammals.

The orange color of carrots, oranges, pumpkins, and other fruits and vegetables comes from the pigment carotene.

Colorants, whether natural or artificial, might be added to the food during processing. Natural colorants come from plants and animals. Plant pigments include red and purple anthocyanins, orange and red carotenoids, green chlorophyll, and yellow flavanols. However, natural fruit and animal pigments tend to be unstable.

Do you think the color of food influences how it tastes? Do certain colors signal sweetness while others signal sourness?

Watch this video to see how food's color might influence whether you think a food is delicious or disgusting!

color impacts the taste of food

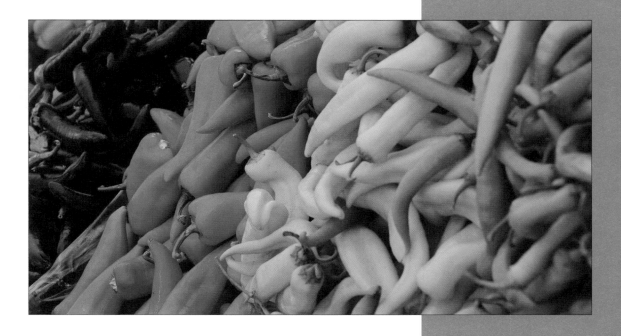

Often, these compounds change and deteriorate more quickly than the food's flavor. Because the color change may give the food a less desirable appearance, it can cause us to reject food that is otherwise safe and full of flavor. Cooking food with heat can also cause the colors in food to fade or change because heat speeds the breakdown of the pigment compounds.

Many food processors add artificial colorants to their food products because **they are more stable and produce brighter colors than many natural pigments.**

Generally, artificial colorants are also stronger, which means less can be used than natural pigments to create a desired color. In a food label, Yellow 5, Blue 1, and Red 40 are examples of artificial colorants.

WHAT'S THAT SMELL?

You look at a bowl of strawberries and decide they look yummy. You grab one and bring it toward your mouth. Before you can take a bite, a sweet smell reaches your nose. It's the strawberry's aroma.

The smell of the strawberry becomes another sensory input that adds to your food experience.

We experience aroma when tiny molecules from a food become airborne and enter the nose. The molecules interact with sensory receptors in the nose and trigger electrical signals to the brain. In the brain, these signals are processed and interpreted as aroma. We smell the strawberry.

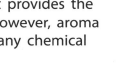

Some foods have a single compound that provides the aroma for the food. A compound in raspberries called raspberry ketone delivers the recognizable raspberry aroma. Benzaldehyde is the compound that provides the aroma of almonds. In most foods, however, aroma is the result of the interaction of many chemical compounds.

TOUCH AND TEXTURE

How do you like your peanut butter—creamy or chunky? What about French fries—crispy or soft? While a food's flavor is important, its texture—crispiness, creaminess, and chewiness—is also an integral part of whether or not you enjoy a dish. If a food doesn't feel right in your hand or mouth, you're probably not going to eat it.

The texture of food influences whether we choose to eat a food and like it or reject the food. If a food is too hard, too mushy, or too chewy, you might not want to eat it.

FOOD FACT

Some substances, such as menthol, peppermint, and camphor, can trigger a fake sensation of cold in the mouth. These substances trigger temperature-sensitive nerves in the mouth even though the actual temperature does not change.

Mushy peas—yea or nay?

A peach that is hard when sliced with a knife might not be appealing. How a piece of steak feels when we cut it or how risotto feels when we stir it with a spoon may influence whether we want to eat the food.

A food's texture describes the properties of a food that are detected by our sense of touch, both in the mouth and with our hands.

Texture is often described as hard, soft, smooth, lumpy, crispy, mushy, creamy, or crunchy.

Food texture is also a signal of quality. As a food is stored, its texture can change. If fruits and vegetables lose water during storage, they wilt and shrivel. Bread loses water and becomes hard and stale. If not stored properly, ice cream can lose its creamy texture and become gritty from the formation of ice crystals.

MOUTHFEEL

In the mouth, food and drink have a distinct feel. They create physical sensations that are separate from taste. These physical sensations are known as mouthfeel. Mouthfeel is a sensory attribute of food, which, along with taste and smell, helps to determine the overall flavor of food.

It's really just like it sounds! Mouthfeel describes the texture of food and drink as felt in the mouth. Take a spoonful of mashed potatoes and run your tongue through it. Are the potatoes smooth or lumpy? Which texture do you prefer?

Getting the texture of food right is a complex process. Have you ever wondered how food scientists use their knowledge of chemistry to create ideal food textures?

Take a look at this video about the science of food texture.

Univar food science texture

When you chew food, the teeth, jaw, and tongue exert forces on the food. How the food responds to these forces determines how you perceive its texture. If the food breaks easily, it may be brittle. If a lot of force is required to break it, the food is hard. If it flows in the mouth, it is runny.

In your mouth, special sensory receptors are sensitive to physical stimuli, such as temperature, pain, touch, and pressure. These mechanoreceptors are similar to others found throughout the body's skin and muscles, but your mouth has a greater density of these receptors compared to other parts of your body. These receptors are attached to nerve fibers that send signals to the brain. They respond to mechanical, chemical, and temperature-related stimuli.

For example, when you drink bubbly soda, receptors in the mouth send signals to the brain that cause a prickling sensation in your mouth. They register if tea is hot or ice cream is cold. The mechanoreceptors also send signals about the size, shape, and coarseness of solids and can detect differences in food texture and vibrations caused by the movements of the tongue and jaws.

MANIPULATING TEXTURE

Because texture is so important to the overall experience of food, getting texture just right is essential. Most people expect a certain texture when they eat a food. If they don't find it, it negatively affects their experience with the food.

CAN YOU FEEL IT?

Texture of a food is subjective. Your friend might love to eat cottage cheese, while you won't touch it, simply because of its texture. Scientists now believe that some people are better able to detect tiny differences in texture because their tongues are better at perceiving food particle sizes. The perception of food texture comes from the interaction of food with mechanoreceptors in the mouth. When the mechanoreceptors are activated, they send an electrical signal through the nervous system to the brain. Those who have more sensitive receptors may be better able to perceive particle size in a food product. What food textures do you like?

Some people love to eat raw oysters. Other people find the thought of swallowing an oyster disgusting.

That's why food companies may add certain carbohydrates and proteins known as texturants to foods. Texturants can impact the texture and mouthfeel of food products with little impact on flavor. Research scientists experiment with blends of different texturants to achieve the desired texture and mouthfeel in a specific food.

Some texturants are thickening agents. They increase the viscosity—the thickness and stickiness—of liquid foods. Thickeners are often used in dairy foods, puddings, dessert fillings, soups, sauces, dressings, and bakery mixes. Many thickeners contain starch molecules that swell in water when cooked and increase the food's viscosity.

Gelling agents transform a liquid mixture into a solid food.

They are typically used in gummy candies, jams, jellies, meats, custards, puddings, spread, and yogurts. Starch gelling agents have starch molecule chains that form a network as the food cools to create the gel.

Other texturants called emulsifiers prevent oil from separating from water in food. Some create a film over a food product, while others are applied to the surface of foods to change their surface appearance. Emulsifiers also reduce stickiness and control crystallization. They are often added to ice cream, margarine, salad dressings, and other creamy sauces to allow oil and water in these foods to be blended into a stable emulsion.

Some texturants called bulking materials increase the carbohydrate solids in a food. Bulking materials help to give low-moisture foods such as cereals and bakery items a desired firmness and denseness.

SIZE AND SHAPE

Even the shape of food can affect how it tastes. When Cadbury changed the shape of its Dairy Milk chocolate bars, customers complained. Unhappy customers sent emails to Cadbury asking why they had changed the recipe for the beloved chocolate bar. They insisted that the new rounder chocolate bar no longer tasted the same. Yet Cadbury had not changed the chocolate recipe at all. Only the bar's shape had changed.

Research into food's shape shows that the customers might have been right. The chocolate bar's new rounder shape caused the bar to melt faster in the mouth. As it melts more quickly, it also releases different flavor compounds at a faster rate. The result: The chocolate tasted different.

ASTRINGENCY

Some food and drink with a high concentration of tannins cause the mouth to feel dry and sticky. Tannins are chemical compounds found in plants, seeds, bark, wood, leaves, and fruit skins. The sensation they give in the mouth is called astringency. The skins of grapes, strong tea, or a green banana can commonly trigger astringency. The sensation of astringency occurs when chemical reactions occur between the food containing tannins and the surface of the tongue and saliva. The tannins bind with proteins in the saliva and cause them to clump together. These clumps thicken the saliva and make it stickier. As a result, the saliva is less able to help food slide over the tongue and past the sides of the mouth. This creates the sensation of a dry and sticky mouth.

- Why do people who work in food processing pay so much attention to the look and feel of food, not just the flavor?

- Why do many foods have lots of additives? How might food be different without preservatives or texturants?

According to scientists who study food shape and flavor, foods with a rounder shape often taste sweeter. Foods with a more angular shape taste bitter. That's why a piece of cake cut in a circle might taste sweeter. And why a curved piece of meat cut into angular pieces may taste saltier and more savory.

The shape of food can also influence how we perceive it.

In the grocery store, many people pass over produce that is not perfectly shaped or sized. Even though they taste the same as more perfect pieces, misshapen strawberries, discolored apples, and undersized potatoes are regularly skipped for fruits and vegetables that look more appealing. Some of these imperfect fruits and vegetables get processed for juice. Others go to food banks. Some remain unused and become waste.

FOOD FACT

Different foods have different textures, such as crisp potato chips, crunchy celery, creamy ice cream, and tender meats.

Cooking a delicious meal is much more than mixing a few ingredients in a bowl. Creating a light and airy cake, a savory steak, or a creamy sauce is a science. Great chefs use the principles of chemistry to create chemical reactions that turn simple ingredients into mouthwatering meals. They use their knowledge of flavors to enhance foods and create new recipes. And they know that presentation matters, as food's color, texture, and shape can take a meal from ho-hum to extraordinary.

Using science, you can turn your next kitchen experiment into an excellent and delicious meal!

TEXT TO WORLD

Is there a food texture that you especially don't like? What about one that you really like? Why?

HOW STARCHES WORK AS THICKENING AGENTS

Thickening agents are added to foods such as dairy products, puddings, soups, and sauces to increase viscosity. Many are made up of starch molecules that absorb water and swell, reducing liquid and thickening the substance. In this activity, you'll test different thickening agents, such as cornstarch, potato starch, tapioca, and arrowroot, and see how they work in food.

CAUTION: Ask an adult for help using the stove.

- **Measure 1 cup of water.** Spoon out 2 tablespoons to a small bowl. Add 2 tablespoons of cornstarch to the bowl and stir. Continue adding 1 tablespoon of water at a time, while stirring, until the cornstarch dissolves. Then, slowly add more cornstarch until the mixture is the consistency of yogurt.

- **Put the water remaining in the measuring cup into a saucepan.** Heat it on a stovetop until it is about 150 degrees Fahrenheit (66 degrees Celsius). Add the cornstarch and water solution and stir until it is dissolved. Continue stirring for seven minutes. Remove from the heat.

- **Test the thickness by propping a cookie sheet at an angle.** Pour one spoonful at the higher end of the sheet. Use a timer to measure how long it takes the solution to reach the bottom of the cookie sheet. Record your measurements and observations in your science journal.

- **Repeat this process with each type of thickening agent.** Record your observations. Which starch worked the best as a thickening agent? Which was the worst? How can you tell?

VOCAB LAB

Write down what you think each word means. What root words can you find to help you? What does the context of the word tell you?

astringency, **emulsifier**, **mechanoreceptor**, **mouthfeel**, **rheology**, **texturant**, and **viscosity**.

Compare your definitions with those of your friends or classmates. Did you all come up with the same meanings? Turn to the text and glossary if you need help.

To investigate more, repeat this experiment without heating the solution. How does heat affect the ability of starch to serve as a thickening agent? Explain your results.

Ideas for Supplies ▼

- 3 glass jars with lids
- vegetable oil
- white vinegar
- food coloring
- eggs

To investigate more, try using the egg yolk instead of the egg white in this experiment. What happens? You can also try using a different type of vinegar. Does this change your results? Why or why not?

EMULSIFIERS: MIXING OIL AND WATER

Left alone with each other, oil and water do not mix. Polar water molecules attract each other and form hydrogen bonds. They cluster together, while the oil's molecules cluster with themselves. However, what happens when you add an emulsifier to the mixture? In this activity, you will explore the role of albumin (the protein found in egg whites) as an emulsifier. An emulsifier is soluble in both fat and water and allows fats to be uniformly spread throughout water as an emulsion. Foods that consist of emulsions include ice cream, salad dressings, mayonnaise, butter, and margarine.

- **Label the jars 1, 2, and 3.** Add ½ cup vegetable oil, ½ cup white vinegar, and one drop of food coloring to each jar. What happens to the food coloring?

- **Separate the yolk and white of an egg and save the parts in separate bowls.** Add 2 tablespoons of egg white to jar #1. Add 2 tablespoons of water to jar #2. Add 1 tablespoon of egg white and 1 tablespoon of water to jar #3.

- **Secure the lids on the jars and shake them to mix the oil and vinegar.** Place the jars on a flat surface and start a timer. For each jar, how long does it take the oil and vinegar to separate and form a clear boundary between the top layer of oil and the bottom layer of vinegar?

- **Which mixture took the shortest amount of time to separate?** Which took the longest? Which jar had the most effective emulsifying agent? How do you know?

HOW DOES COLOR INFLUENCE FLAVOR?

Does the color of food and drink influence how people perceive flavor? Let's try an experiment to find out! You'll need a flavored clear liquid such as a lemon-lime soda or clear sports drink to start.

- **Divide the clear liquid into four cups.**

- **Add food coloring to three of the cups: red food coloring in one cup, yellow in the second cup, and purple in the third cup.** Leave the liquid in the fourth cup clear. Mix each well.

- **Pour the colored drinks into four small tasting cups, one set for each volunteer.** Have volunteers taste each one, but don't tell them it is the same drink. Ask the volunteers, which one tastes the sweetest? Which one tastes the sourest? Which one is the least appealing?

- **Repeat the process with vanilla pudding.** Add different food colorings and taste test with volunteers. Which pudding do they think tastes the sweetest? Which tastes the sourest? Which is the least appealing?

- **What do your results say about how color affects perception of flavor?**

> To investigate more, try additional colors and test how they affect taste perception. What about the shape of food? Design an experiment to test how different shapes affect perception of taste.

Ideas for Supplies ▼

- clear liquid
- several large cups
- several small cups
- food coloring
- vanilla pudding
- several bowls
- spoons

CRISPY OVEN-FRIED POTATOES

Oven-baked potatoes are a delicious side dish for many meals. How can you make these potatoes extra crispy and satisfying? In this activity, we'll compare two methods of making oven-fried potatoes and see which makes the crispiest bites.

CAUTION: Ask an adult for help using the oven.

Ingredients ▼

- 2 baking potatoes
- 2 tablespoons olive oil
- 1 teaspoon salt

- **Wash the potatoes thoroughly.** Then, cut them lengthwise into wedges of approximately the same size.

- **Separate the wedges into two piles.** For each wedge in one pile, cut a small, triangular notch on the side without skin so you can tell them apart. Dry the wedges and place this pile in a bowl.

- **Take the second pile of wedges and submerge them in cold water for 20 minutes.** Then, drain the wedges and pat dry.

- **Preheat the oven to 450 degrees Fahrenheit.** Toss all of the potato wedges with 2 tablespoons of olive oil and 1 teaspoon of salt.

- **Spread the wedges in a single layer on a baking sheet.** Bake for 10 minutes. Turn the wedges over and bake for 10 more minutes. Continue baking and turning until the wedges are golden brown.

- **Pick three wedges with notches and three without notches to test.** Create a data table for your results.

  - What color are they?
  - How do they smell?
  - Do they snap into two pieces or bend?
  - Which method of cooking produced the crispiest potatoes? Why?

To investigate more, choose another vegetable to oven fry. How do your results compare to what you discovered with the potatoes? What are the differences between the new vegetable and the original potatoes? How do you think the chemical makeup of each influenced your results?

absorb: to soak up.

acid: a substance that has a pH less than 7.

activation energy: the energy that starts a chemical reaction.

additive: a substance added to something in small quantities to improve or preserve it.

alkaline: having a pH greater than 7.

amino acid: an organic compound composed of nitrogen, carbon, hydrogen and oxygen, along with a variable side chain group that are the building blocks of proteins.

aroma: a distinctive smell.

artery: a blood vessel that carries blood from the heart to the rest of the body.

artificial: manmade.

artificial colorant: a human-made dye, pigment, or other substance that colors something.

artificial flavorant: a human-made substance that adds flavor to food.

astringency: slight acidity or bitterness of taste or smell.

atom: the smallest particle of matter that cannot be broken down by chemical means. An atom is made up of a nucleus of protons and neutrons surrounded by a cloud of electrons.

atomic: about or relating to atoms.

ATP: adenosine triphosphate. A compound that provides energy for cell and body processes.

attract: to pull things closer together.

aversion: having a strong dislike of something.

bacteria: tiny organisms found in animals, plants, soil, and water that help decay food. Some bacteria are harmful and others are helpful.

base: a substance that has a pH greater than 7.

biology: the study of life and of living organisms.

bitter: having a sharp, pungent taste or smell; not sweet.

bond: a force that holds together the atoms or groups of atoms in a molecule or crystal.

browning reaction: a chemical reaction that causes food to develop a golden-brown color.

byproduct: a secondary product made in the manufacture of something else.

calcium: a mineral necessary for life.

caramelization: a chemical reaction that occurs when sugars are heated, which causes a golden-brown color and nutty flavors in food.

carbohydrate: one of the essential food nutrients, which includes sugars and starches.

carbon: an element found in all organic compounds.

carbon dioxide: a gas formed by the burning of fossil fuels, the rotting of plants and animals, and the breathing out of animals, including humans.

carotene: a naturally occurring pigment found in carrots and other plants.

catalyst: a material that increases the rate of a chemical reaction without being consumed in the reaction.

cell: the most basic part of a living thing. Billions of cells make up a plant or animal, while other organisms are single-celled.

cellular respiration: the process by which the body turns glucose into energy that can be used to power cell processes.

chemesthesis: a chemical sensitivity of the skin and mucous membranes.

chemical: the pure form of a substance. Some chemicals can be combined or broken up to create new chemicals.

chemical bond: the attraction between atoms, ions, or molecules that allows the formation of chemical compounds.

GLOSSARY

chemical reaction: a process where one or more substances are chemically changed and transformed into different substances.

chemistry: the study of the properties of substances and how they react with one another.

cholesterol: a waxy, fatlike substance that is found in all cells of the body.

chronic: recurring.

classify: to put things in groups based on what they have in common.

coagulation: the change in the structure of a protein from a liquid form to a thicker liquid or solid brought about by heat, stirring, or acid.

collagen: a family of proteins that are the primary structural component of connective tissues, such as skin and cartilage.

colorant: a pigment that gives color to a substance.

complementary protein: a protein that, when paired with another protein, provides all of the essential amino acids needed by the human body in adequate proportions.

complete protein: a protein that provides all of the essential amino acids needed by the human body in adequate proportions.

composition: the ingredients in a mixture or substance.

compound: a pure substance made of two or more elements in specific proportions.

concentration: the amount of a substance in relation to others.

condense: to change from a gas to a liquid.

conduction: the transfer of heat or energy from one substance to another through direct contact.

convection: the transfer of heat by the movement of a fluid (liquid or gas) between areas of different temperature.

cortisol: a hormone produced in response to stress.

covalent bond: a type of chemical bond that involves sharing a pair of electrons between atoms.

cranial nerve: any of the 12 paired nerves that originate in the brain stem.

cream: to mash together butter and sugar to create a light and fluffy mixture.

crystal: a solid with its atoms arranged in a geometric pattern.

crystallize: to form crystals.

dehydrated: when the body does not have enough water and other fluids to carry out its normal functions.

denaturation: to change the molecular structure of something, such as causing proteins to unfold and lose their shape.

dense: how tightly the matter in an object is packed.

digestive system: the system in the body responsible for receiving and digesting food, absorbing the nutrients, and eliminating what is not needed.

dilute: to make a liquid thinner by adding water to it.

dissolve: to break up or be absorbed by a solvent.

distill: to separate a mixture based on differing boiling points.

DNA: deoxyribonucleic acid. The substance found in your cells that carries your genes, the genetic information that contains the blueprint of who you are.

electrical charge: a property of matter. Protons have a positive charge and electrons have a negative charge.

electrolytes: essential minerals, including sodium, calcium, and potassium, that are vital to many key functions in the body.

electromagnetic: one of the fundamental forces of the universe, which is responsible for magnetic attraction and electrical charges.

electron: a negatively charged particle that is found in orbitals outside the nucleus of an atom.

element: a substance that cannot be broken down into simpler substances.

emulsifier: a substance that stabilizes an emulsion, such as a food additive used to stabilize processed foods.

emulsion: a mixture of two liquids that are usually unmixable.

endothermic: a reaction that needs energy to take place.

enzyme: a catalyst in biochemical reactions.

essential amino acids: amino acids that cannot be made by the human body.

essential fats: fatty acids that must be consumed because they cannot be made by the human body.

essential vitamins: vitamins that are required for the functioning of the human body.

evaporate: to convert from a liquid to a gas.

exothermic: a reaction that generates energy in the form of heat.

extracted: removed or taken out by effort or force.

fat: one of the three main macronutrients, along with proteins and carbohydrates, that are necessary for the functioning of the human body.

fat-soluble: a substance that can be dissolved in fats.

fatty acid: any of a class of acids that form part of a lipid molecule. Fatty acids are simple molecules built around a series of carbon atoms linked together in a chain that occur naturally in animal and vegetable fats and oils.

fiber: a type of carbohydrate from the cell walls of plants that the body cannot digest.

filter: to pass a liquid through something to remove unwanted material.

flavor: a distinctive taste and smell of a food or drink.

flavor compounds: the chemical compounds in a food that contribute to its flavor.

flavorant: a chemical compound that adds flavor to food.

food scientist: a chemist who studies food.

force: a push or pull that changes an object's motion.

fructose: a type of sugar commonly found in fruit.

gel: a mixture formed when water molecules are spread in a solid substance.

gelatinization: the process where starch and water are heated, which causes the starch granules to swell.

gelling agent: food additives used to thicken and stabilize various foods, such as jellies, desserts and candies.

genetic: relating to genes, which are units of DNA and RNA that assign organisms their characteristics.

gland: an organ in the body that makes and releases substances the body needs.

glucose: a simple sugar that is an important energy source in living organisms and is a component of many carbohydrates.

gluten: a protein formed from flour and water.

glycogen: a form of glucose with several glucose molecules stuck together.

glycolysis: the first step of cellular respiration in which molecules of glucose are broken down by enzymes, releasing energy and pyruvic acid.

helix: a shape like a spiral staircase.

hemoglobin: a substance in red blood cells that combines with and carries oxygen around the body and gives blood its red color.

GLOSSARY

homogenous: something that is completely mixed with a uniform composition.

hormones: chemical messengers in the human body.

hydrogen bond: a weak bond between two molecules.

hydrolysis: the chemical breakdown of a compound due to reaction with water.

immune system: the system that protects the body against disease and infection.

incomplete protein: a protein that provides some, but not all, of the essential amino acids required by the body.

inflammation: a physical condition in which part of the body becomes reddened, swollen, hot, and often painful, especially as a reaction to injury or infection.

inorganic: a compound that does not contain carbon. Also refers to something not living.

insulin: a hormone made by the pancreas that allows the body to use sugar (glucose) from carbohydrates in food for energy or to store glucose for future use.

interact: how things that are together affect each other.

intermolecular: existing or acting between molecules.

ion: a particle with either a positive or negative charge.

ionic bond: a type of chemical bond that transfers an electron from one atom to another.

keratin: a protein used in nails and hair.

kinetic energy: energy caused by an object's motion.

Krebs cycle: the second step in cellular respiration, a series of chemical reactions to release stored energy.

leavening agent: a substance that causes the expansion of doughs and batters by the release of gases within them. Examples of leavening agents include yeast, baking soda, and baking powder.

lipid: a fat, one of the body's three main macronutrients, which provides energy and is essential for many body processes.

macro mineral: a mineral needed in larger quantities for the human body to function.

macronutrients: one of three main nutrients— carbohydrates, lipids, and proteins—necessary for the human body to function and grow.

Maillard reaction: a chemical reaction between amino acids and sugars in food that produces a brown color and new flavors.

matter: any material or substance that takes up space.

mechanoreceptors: receptors in the mouth and skin that sense physical stimuli such as touch.

melting point: the temperature at which a solid changes into a liquid.

menthol: a chemical compound that produces a cooling sensation and is found in peppermint and other natural oils.

metabolism: a set of chemical reactions within the cells of living things that allow them to grow, reproduce, maintain their structure, and respond to the environment.

micronutrients: vitamins and minerals needed by the body in small quantities every day.

microorganism: a living thing so small that it can be seen only with a microscope.

minerals: nutrients found in rocks and soil that keep plants and animals healthy and growing. Salt and nitrogen are two minerals.

mixture: a substance created by two or more substances that are combined physically but not chemically.

molecule: a group of atoms covalently bonded together, the simplest structural unit of an element or compound. Molecules can break apart and form new ones, which is a chemical reaction.

mouthfeel: the physical sensations of food and drink in the mouth.

myoglobin: a protein in meat that produces a red-purple color.

nasopharynx: the upper part of the pharynx, which connects the nose, mouth, and esophagus.

natural colorant: a pigment that is extracted from a natural source and gives color to a substance.

natural flavorant: a compound that gives another substance flavor and is extracted from a natural source.

nerve fibers: long, slender projections of a nerve cell or neuron, which carries electrical impulses from the nerve through the nervous system.

nervous system: the communication system of the body, made of nerve cells that connect the brain and extend through the body.

neurological: relating to the brain and the nervous system.

neuron: a special cell that sends electrical and chemical messages to your brain.

neutron: a particle in the nucleus of an atom that does not have a charge.

nucleus: the center of an atom, which holds protons and neutrons.

nutrient: a substance that provides nourishment essential for growth and the maintenance of life.

nutrition: the study of nutrients in food, how the body uses them, and the relationship between diet, health, and disease.

oils: a type of lipid that is usually in liquid form.

olfactory: relating to or connected with the sense of smell.

oral cavity: the cavity of the mouth.

orbit: a repeating path that circles around something else.

organ: a body part that has a certain function, such as the heart or kidneys.

organic: a type of compound that contains the element carbon and often hydrogen, as well as other elements. Refers to something that is living.

organism: any living thing.

papillae: small bumps on the tongue that hold taste buds.

particle: an extremely small piece of something.

perception: the ability to interpret information from the senses.

periodic table: a chart that shows the chemical elements arranged according to their properties.

pH: a scale used to tell the acidity of a solution, with the value of 7 being neutral.

phase transition: the change of matter from one state to another, such as solid to liquid or liquid to gas.

phases: the three states of matter: solid, liquid, and gas.

physics: the science of how matter and energy work together.

pigment: a substance that gives color to something.

polar molecule: a molecule that has a positively charged end and a negatively charged end. A water molecule is an example of a polar molecule.

precipitate: a solid created from a chemical reaction in a solution.

preservative: an additive to food.

GLOSSARY

process: an activity that takes several steps to complete.

processed food: food that has been manufactured rather than grown naturally or prepared at home. It has added ingredients to make it look nicer, taste better, last longer, or cost less.

product: a substance created by a chemical reaction.

properties: characteristic qualities or distinctive features of something.

proportions: the balanced relationships between parts of a whole.

protein: one of three main macronutrients essential for the body to function and grow. Proteins are one of the building blocks of body tissue and can also serve as a fuel source.

protein denaturation: a process in which proteins unfold and lose their shape.

proton: a positively charged particle in the nucleus of an atom.

pure: a substance in which all of the molecules are the same.

puree: a smooth, creamy substance made of liquidized or crushed fruit or vegetables.

radiant heat: a type of heat transfer in which electromagnetic waves penetrate an object and cause its molecules to vibrate, which generates heat.

rancid: a fat or oil that smells or tastes unpleasant because it is old or stale.

rate of reaction: the speed of a chemical reaction.

ratio: the relationship in size or quantity between two or more things.

react: to change in response to a stimulus.

reactant: a substance involved in and changed by a chemical reaction.

receptor: a cell or group of cells that receives stimuli.

renaturation: the reconstruction of a protein to its original form, especially after denaturation.

repel: to force away or apart.

RNA: ribonucleic acid, the genetic material that contains the code to make a certain protein.

respiration: the act of breathing, a process in living organisms that involves the production of energy, typically with the intake of oxygen and the release of carbon dioxide.

rheology: the study of food's texture and how it reacts when a force is applied to it.

saliva: the watery liquid secreted into the mouth by glands, providing lubrication for chewing and swallowing and aiding digestion.

salivation: the act or process of producing saliva.

saturated fats: dietary fats that are often solid at room temperature.

sauté: to cook in a shallow pan with a small amount of oil or fat over high heat.

savory: one of the five tastes. Also called umami.

sensory: relating to or perceived by the senses.

shell: the area in which an electron moves around an atom's nucleus.

smell: one of the five senses; the perception of air-borne molecules through sensory receptors in the nose.

solute: the substance that is dissolved in a solution.

solution: a homogenous liquid mixture.

solvent: the substance that dissolves a solute.

spoilage: rotting or rotted.

stabilizer: something that acts to hold matter steady.

stable: steady.

starch: a type of carbohydrate that is made from many sugar molecules bonded together. Starches take longer to digest than simple sugars.

stimulus: a change in an organism's environment that causes an action, activity, or response. Plural is stimuli.

substance: the physical material from which something is made.

sucrose: a type of simple sugar, also known as white table sugar.

sugar: a type of carbohydrate that is easily broken down by the body and used for quick energy.

supertaster: a person who experiences taste more strongly than the average person.

surface area: a measure of the total area that the surface of an object occupies.

synthetic: something not found in nature, made of artificial materials using a chemical reaction.

tannins: bitter-tasting chemical compounds found in plants, seeds, bark, wood, leaves, and fruit skins.

taste: one of the five senses, the sensation of flavor produced by receptors in the mouth and throat.

taste aversion: the avoidance of a certain food after the association of an illness or other unpleasant event with it.

taste buds: sensory organs that are found on the tongue. They hold the taste receptor cells that allow a person to experience sweet, salty, bitter, sour, and savory tastes.

taste receptors: sensory cells on the tongue, mouth, and throat that detect sweet, salty, biter, sour, and savory tastes.

temperature: a measure of the average energy or speed, of all of the particles in a substance.

tenderize: to make meat more tender.

texturant: a food additive that changes the texture and feel of a food.

texture: the feel, appearance, or consistency of a substance.

thickening agent: a food additive that increases the viscosity—thickness and stickiness—of a food or liquid.

toxic: poisonous.

trace mineral: a mineral needed in small quantities for the growth and development of the human body.

trans fats: unhealthy fats in food produced by a process that turns healthy oils into solids. Trans fats have been linked to several diseases and are banned in the United States and many countries.

umami: a savory flavor.

uniform: always the same.

unsaturated fats: healthy, essential fats that have one or more double bonds connecting their carbon chains.

vapor: a gas.

vibrate: to move or cause to move continuously and rapidly back and forth.

viscosity: the resistance to flow of a fluid.

vitamins: organic substances found in food that the body needs to grow and develop normally.

volatile: something likely to change quickly and unpredictably.

volume: the amount of space inside an object.

water vapor: the gas state of water.

RESOURCES

BOOKS

Acids and Bases: Food Chemistry for Kids Children's Chemistry Books. Baby Professor, 2017.

Brown, Cynthia Light. *Kitchen Chemistry: Cool Crystals, Rockin' Reactions, and Magical Mixtures with Hands-On Science Activities.* Nomad Press, 2020.

Schloss, Andrew. *Amazing (Mostly) Edible Science: A Family Guide to Fun Experiments in the Kitchen.* Quarry Books, 2016.

Hartings, Matthew. *Chemistry in Your Kitchen.* Royal Society of Chemistry, 2017.

Parker, Lucie. *Exploring Kitchen Science: 30+ Edible Experiments & Kitchen Activities.* Weldon Owen, 2015.

Heinecke, Liz Lee. *Kitchen Science for Kids: 26 Family-Friendly Experiments for Fun Around the House.* Quarry Books, 2018.

How Science Works: The Facts Visually Explained. DK Publishing, 2018.

Gray, Theodore. *Molecules: The Elements and the Architecture of Everything.* Black Dog & Leventhal Publishers, 2014.

WEBSITES

Academy of Nutrition and Dietetics
eatright.org

American Chemical Society: Food and Cooking Chemistry
acs.org/content/acs/en/education/students/highschool/
chemistryclubs/activities/food-and-chemistry

Chemistry for Kids
sciencekids.co.nz/chemistry.html

Harvard School of Public Health: The Nutrition Source
hsph.harvard.edu/nutritionsource

Middle School Chemistry
middleschoolchemistry.com

Nutrition.gov
nutrition.gov

Radar's Chem4Kid
chem4kids.com

University of Georgia: Science Behind Our Food: Chemistry
extension.uga.edu/programs-services/science-behind-our-food.html

METRIC CONVERSIONS

Use this chart to find the metric equivalents to the English measurements in this activity. If you need to know a half measurement, divide by two. If you need to know twice the measurement, multiply by two.

ENGLISH	METRIC	
1 inch	2.5	centimeters
1 foot	30.5	centimeters
1 yard	0.9	meter
1 mile	1.6	kilometers
1 pound	0.5	kilogram
1 teaspoon	5	milliliters
1 tablespoon	15	milliliters
1 cup	237	milliliters

RESOURCES

SELECTED BIBLIOGRAPHY

Copeland, Les. "The Chemical Reactions That Make Food Taste Awesome," *Discover Magazine*, June 3, 2016.

Crosby, Guy. *Cooks Science*. America's Test Kitchen, 2016.

Depa, Vaclavik V., and E.W. Christian. *Essentials of Food Science, 4th Edition*. Springer, 2014.

Field, Simon. *Culinary Reactions: The Everyday Chemistry of Cooking*. Chicago Review, 2012.

McGee, Harold. *On Food and Cooking: The Science and Lore of the Kitchen*. Scribner, 2007.

Mouritsen, Ole G., and Klavs Styrbæk. *Mouthfeel: How Texture Makes Taste*. Columbia University Press, 2018.

Özilgen, Z.S. *Cooking As a Chemical Reaction: Culinary Science with Experiments*. CRC Press, 2020.

Potter, Jeff. *Cooking for Geeks: Real Science, Great Cooks, and Good Food*. O'Reilly Media, 2016.

"The Science of Taste," International Food Information Council Foundation, March 13, 2018. foodinsight.org

Shewfelt, Robert L., Alicia Orta-Ramirez, and Andrew D. Clarke. *Introducing Food Science*. CRC Press 2017.

QR CODE GLOSSARY

Page 9: youtube.com/watch?v=2P_0HGRWgXw&list=PLtLT74crQcwXifCszpuk21I4ye3ghf-kV&index=5&t=0s

Page 23: laughingsquid.com/why-hard-boiled-egg-yolks-turn-green

Page 27: youtube.com/watch?v=inEPlZZ_SfA

Page 35: youtube.com/watch?v=Ndmebd5u-EA

Page 38: youtube.com/watch?v=v62ilJCaMFk

Page 39: youtube.com/watch?v=oiGUyvMHqM4

Page 40: youtube.com/watch?v=c7WI41huAok

Page 48: youtube.com/watch?v=p0dLwCP61Vw

Page 62: youtube.com/watch?v=V_E7mq8bv4g

Page 64: youtube.com/watch?v=_15eUNiH0eA

Page 66: ed.ted.com/lessons/what-is-fat-george-zaidan

Page 70: ed.ted.com/lessons/how-your-digestive-system-works-emma-bryce

Page 81: youtube.com/watch?v=Qmip5rYPx0s

Page 82: youtube.com/watch?v=LVg_ypwNqho

Page 85: youtube.com/watch?v=W7Pzhvypg9A

Page 95: youtube.com/watch?v=waFOTNleAuc

Page 98: youtube.com/watch?v=j7qwnmMn9mo

INDEX

INDEX

N

neurogastronomy, 100
neutrons, 4
nitrogen, 7, 24, 40
nutrition, 59–74
    carbohydrates for,
      60, 64–65, 71
    chemical reaction effects on, 42
    definition of, 60
    digestion of nutrients, 68–70
    energy from, 70–72
    essential nutrients, 27
    fats for, 60, 66
    proteins for, 60, 61–63
    vitamins and minerals for,
      vii, 25–27, 60, 61
    water for, 60, 67, 68

O

oils and fats. *See* lipids, fats, oils
omega-3 fatty acids, 21, 66
oxygen, 7, 11, 17, 22, 24, 71

P

Pauling, Linus, vii
periodic table, vi, viii–ix, 12
preservatives, 27–28, 30, 90
proteins. *See also* enzymes
    denaturation and coagulation,
      42–43, 46, 49, 50–51
    flavor of, 85
    in foods, 16, 18, 23–24
    genetically engineered, vii
    nutrition from, 60, 61–63
    texture with, 100
protons, 4–5, 11
Pure Food and Drug Act, vi

R

refrigeration, 8, 44
rheology, 99
Rutherford, Ernest, vi

S

salt, 6, 8, 23, 27, 28, 58, 72, 83
saltiness, vii, 79, 82, 83, 88, 102
saturated fats, 20–21
savory taste, vi, vii, 23,
    82, 84, 87, 102
scientific method, 5
smell, 75–77, 80–82, 88, 91, 96–97
solutions, 7–8, 18
sourness, 46, 79, 82,
    84–85, 88, 95
spoilage, vii, 8, 24, 27–28,
    44, 79, 85
starches, 22–23, 39, 45,
    64, 100–101, 103. *See
    also* carbohydrates
sugars
    artificial, vii
    caramelization of, 11–12,
      39, 40, 49, 52–53
    chemical formula, 7
    flavor of, 83–84
    in food, 22, 27, 45
    hydrolysis of, 43
    Maillard reaction, 40–42, 49
    nutrition from, 64–65, 71, 72
    solutions, 8
sulfur, 23, 27, 40
supertasters, 85
sweetness, vii, 22, 23, 79, 82,
    83–84, 86–88, 95, 102

T

tannins, 101
taste, vi, vii, 22, 75–79, 81–88.
    See also flavor; *specific tastes*
texture, 93–106
    appearance and, 94–96, 105
    manipulation of,
      99–101, 103–104
    mouthfeel of, 98–99
    size, shape and, 101–102
    smell and, 96–97
    touch and, 97–98
thickening agents, 100–101, 103
Thomson, J.J., vi
toxins, 26, 27, 70, 85, 89
trans fats, vii, 20

U

umami (savory), vi, vii, 23,
    82, 84, 87, 102
unsaturated fats, 21, 66

V

vitamins and minerals,
    vii, 25–27, 60, 61

W

water
    chemical formula, 8, 9, 17
    in food, 16, 17–18, 24, 43
    heating of, 36–37, 38
    hydrolysis with, 43
    nutrition from, 60, 67, 68
    oil and, 19, 29, 101, 104
    solutions, 8, 18
    states of, 10, 18

Y

yeasts, vii, 45, 48